"Phobias are present everywhere and Duane Brown's book can help countless people."

—C.A. Charles "Bud" Baldridge, retired American
Airlines captain

"An outstanding book. I find myself recommending *Flying Without Fear* to nervous flyers on a daily basis."

—Tim Touchet, flight attendant since 1986

"The book addresses all aspects of the fear of flying, from the anxiety that starts days or weeks prior to the flight to touchdown, with techniques to overcome anxiety during each phase. The question and answer format of the book allows a fearful flyer to quickly turn to the section of the book that references their fear and review the strategy they need to use."

—Sheryl Pacelli, former client

flying without fear

SECOND EDITION

Effective Strategies to

Get You Where You Need to Go

DUANE BROWN, PH.D.

New Harbinger Publications, Inc.

Publisher's Note

Distributed in Canada by Raincoast Books

Copyright © 2009 by Duane Brown
New Harbinger Publications, Inc.
5674 Shattuck Avenue
Oakland, CA 94609
www.newharbinger.com

FSC
Mixed Sources
Product group from well-managed
forests and other controlled sources

Cert no. SW-COC-002283
www.fsc.org
© 1996 Forest Stewardship Council

All Rights Reserved
Printed in the United States of America

Acquired by Tesilya Hanauer; Cover design by Amy Shoup; Edited by Elisabeth Beller

Library of Congress Cataloging-in-Publication Data

Brown, Duane.
  Flying without fear : effective strategies to get you where you need to go / Duane Brown.
-- 2nd ed.
     p. cm.
  Includes bibliographical references.
  ISBN-13: 978-1-57224-704-8 (pbk. : alk. paper)
  ISBN-10: 1-57224-704-5 (pbk. : alk. paper) 1. Fear of flying. I. Title.
  RC1090.B76 2009
  616.85'225--dc22

                              2009023476

11 10 09   10 9 8 7 6 5 4 3 2 1   First printing

Contents

Acknowledgments

No author can claim expertise in all of the areas covered in *Flying Without Fear*. I am particularly indebted to Captain Steve Fryer for his assistance with the technical aspects of the first edition. Captain Charles "Bud" Baldridge filled the same role in the preparation of this edition. Both Steve and Bud are now retired. American Airlines lost two of the best when they left the cockpit.

Tim Touchete began his career as a flight attendant with American Airlines. He now flies with Southwest Airlines. We were recently reminded of the importance of flight attendants to the safety of the passengers when US Airways flight 1549 landed in the freezing waters of the Hudson River. A skilled captain and a crew of well-schooled flight attendants saved every life on that plane. Tim knows safety, and when he spots a fearful flyer aboard one of his flights, he becomes a cheerleader, hand-holder, and dispenser of sage advice. His thoughts regarding this book are much appreciated.

Thanks also go to Sheryl Pacelli, a formal fearful flyer, who took the first step away from the oppression of fear a few years ago and still flies with confidence. This book was written with the goal of freeing others from their debilitating fear of flying.

The editorial staff of New Harbinger deserves much credit for the final product, and my heartfelt thanks go out to them.

Finally, my wife conquered her fear over twenty years ago and was so amazed by the changes it brought about in her life that she immediately set out to establish a fearful flyer program. The American Airlines AAirBorn program came about because of her efforts. Thousands of fearful flyers have benefited as a result. This book is based on the curriculum used in that course.

CHAPTER 1

Flying After 9/11

On September 11, 2001, the world as we knew it in the United States changed forever. At 8:46 A.M. (EDT), hijacked American Airlines Flight 11 was flown into the North Tower of the World Trade Center in New York City. Minutes later, United Airlines Flight 175 flew a similar trajectory into the South Tower of the World Trade Center. Less than an hour after the second attack on the World Trade Center, American Airlines Flight 77 crashed into the Pentagon in Arlington, Virginia. The fourth hijacked flight, United Flight 93, which was destined for either the White House or the Capitol Building in Washington, DC, crashed into an open field near Shanksville, Pennsylvania, thanks to the bravery of its passengers.

Nearly three thousand people died on September 11, 2001, and people who were unafraid of air travel, nervous fliers, and those already convinced that air travel was unsafe asked how this could happen. These same people now ask, "Could it happen again?" This is a valid question, one that cannot be answered with a yes or no. I'll simply say at this point that the answer is probably not, and as time passes, the likelihood will lessen. Good things are in the works. I have faith in the U.S. airline industry and the men and women who fly and repair the planes, serve the passengers, and work to maintain order and safety on the ground.

In the late 1980s and early 1990s, my wife, Sandra, and I headed the American Airlines–sponsored program AAirBorn, which was designed to help fearful fliers overcome their fear. I also saw several people in a part-time private practice while I was a professor at the University of North Carolina at Chapel Hill. More than three thousand people enrolled in the AAirBorn program, and about 85 percent of them received the help they needed. Perhaps more importantly, I was on dozens of flights, sat in on numerous safety briefings, and visited the American Airlines maintenance facility in Tulsa, Oklahoma, where its planes are totally disassembled and refitted as one step in a rigorous maintenance process. I was, as I am now, confident that flying is the safest form of travel. (Support for this claim is provided in chapter 10.)

I was right about the relative safety of air travel and I produced the statistics to prove it in my 1996 book *Flying Without Fear*. However, I was naïve because I didn't incorporate some of the facts that I learned inadvertently into my perspective about air travel. I should have known that some of the incidents I observed could have implications for the aircraft safety. For example, we often conducted fearful flier seminars in New York's LaGuardia Airport. It was not uncommon to find homeless people in secure areas, supposedly accessible only to airline personnel. It never occurred to me that one of those homeless people might plant a bomb in the terminal or infiltrate and hijack an aircraft. When I visited San Diego International Airport, which had the most vigilant security system that I encountered, I learned that a person had been able to climb a chain-link fence surrounding the airport, find a nook on the outside of a plane (probably a wheel well), and take a successful flight. What if that person had been a suicide bomber?

Terrorism was far from my thoughts until September 11, 2001. Metal detectors were in use in New York's LaGuardia Airport, but I learned that they were not as sensitive to the presence of metal as were the metal detectors in Canada. When I flew a return flight with a group of fearful fliers from Montreal to New York, many people in our group found themselves having to remove jewelry, shoes and belts that had metal buckles, and other items that had not been picked up by metal detectors in the United States. Clearly the metal detectors used at Boston's Logan Airport on September 11, 2001, were not sensitive enough to pick up the minuscule metal portion of a box cutter. I also knew that, for the most part, passengers' luggage went uninspected unless they were entering the country or traveling to Israel. When the issue of luggage inspection arose, the main concern seemed to be detecting drugs and identifying illegal purchases that required duty payments, not locating contraband such as explosives. That has changed, as will be shown in chapter 7.

No one that I talked to about safety seemed to realize that a 9/11-type of attack was possible. I was among that group. I was most concerned about the possibility of a bomb being placed aboard an airline in passenger luggage and I made numerous inquiries about this possibility. In 1988, Pan Am Flight 103 was blasted out of the skies over Lockerbie, Scotland, by a bomb. Two hundred and seventy people died. In the late 1980s and the early 1990s, some luggage was x-rayed, but there seemed to be no sense of urgency among airline officials, airport operators, or the Federal Aviation Administration (FAA), the agency that oversees the airline industry. I will say that there was one group that was concerned about the bomb threat: the pilots. Admittedly my sample was limited to a dozen American Airline pilots that I worked with in the AAirBorn program, but they realized that bombs were a real threat to the airplanes they were flying.

The four airliners that crashed because of terrorist attacks on September 11, 2001, eliminated the naïveté about air travel forever. The resulting changes have not made air travel perfectly safe. If you are seeking an unequivocally safe means of transportation, I have one bit of advice for you: stay home! Actually that may not work either. Nearly a dozen people in the Lockerbie, Scotland, area were killed by falling debris when the 747 was blown apart. In the November 12, 2001, crash of American Airlines Flight 587 in New York City, five people were killed on the ground.

Traditionally there has been a tug of war between the airline industry and the agencies that regulate their functioning. Regulations that require additional pilot training or maintenance procedures cost money. It is a beleaguered industry and some companies are on the edge of bankruptcy. Each day meetings are held to find means of cutting expenses. We have already seen salary cuts for most personnel, offshoring of airplane maintenance, elimination of meals and snacks, and extra charges for checked luggage. These cuts raise irrational questions in the mind of the fearful flier and the greater flying public: Are employees disgruntled as a result of the salary cuts? Will they be as diligent in their work because they are performing the same tasks for less money? Will cutting the fat reach the bone in key areas such as maintenance and pilot training? The airline industry could not survive if it was staffed by disgruntled, poorly paid employees who cut corners and jeopardize the safety of passengers who foot the bills. The oversight by the FAA and others is sufficient to ensure the safety of air travel, but one other group is concerned about safety as well. The labor union that represents the pilots lobbies continuously with the FAA, Congress, and the industry to ensure that safety standards are maintained. No pilot wants to strap him- or herself into an unsafe airplane.

FEARFUL FLIER, YOU ARE NOT ALONE

My goal is to update and extend the information presented in the first edition of this book, which targeted fearful fliers. How many of you are there? The National Institute of Mental Health (NIMH) estimates that at any given time, 8.7 percent of nearly two hundred and fifty million in this country, or nearly twenty million adults in the U.S. population, have some type of specific phobia (NIMH 2004). The NIMH estimates are not broken down by type, but my experience suggests that fearful fliers with phobias typically fall into four categories: *aerophobia* (fear of flying), *claustrophobia* (fear of cramped, enclosed spaces), *acrophobia* (fear of heights), and *agoraphobia* (fear of having a panic attack, especially in public, and not being able to escape or get help). However, not all fearful fliers suffer from one of these phobias. Many fearful fliers simply do not have accurate information about pilots, airplanes, air traffic control, and so forth. Some fearful fliers travel by air while others avoid airplanes altogether. Those who do fly often resort to extreme measures such as taking a half-dozen antianxiety pills (e.g., alprazolam, lorazepam) or drinking numerous cocktails, sometimes with disastrous consequences such as the development of alcoholism or drug addiction. Hopefully this small volume will help you take the first step to flying with confidence.

OVERVIEW

I am writing this book at this time primarily because many aspects of the first edition are out of date. Additionally, many people who have read *Flying Without Fear* have contacted me, urging me to write about the threat of terrorism.

In the next chapter, I will ask you to begin to think about the nature of your fear. Some mental health professionals believe that the type of problem that you have is of little consequence when deciding on a treatment strategy. There was a time when I would have subscribed to this philosophy. However, after having dealt with fearful fliers who have a variety of issues, I have come to realize that some fearful fliers need only information while others need far more extensive interventions. Those people who need information may be able to eliminate their fear using the information in chapters 5–7. Others who have phobias will need to read the entire book, and a few will require the help of a skilled therapist to overcome their fear.

Chapter 7 is new to this edition and deals with terrorism and what is being done to combat this threat. You will be relieved to know that there is much in the works as the FAA and Transportation Security Administration (TSA) work to make the U.S. system the best in the world. You can judge for yourself whether this is being accomplished. I'll compare the U.S. system with the one employed by El Al, the national airline of Israel, which has the best existing security system in the world.

I've already said that fearful fliers with psychological problems will need more than information. It would be difficult for them to overcome their fear using self-help procedures, but I have seen it done. Chapters 2–4 may be useful in self-curative attempts. These chapters duplicate the procedures I used in my private practice. Other mental health professionals will undoubtedly use other approaches. Chapters 8, 9, and 11 should be helpful to almost every flier who has some degree of anxiety. Chapter 8 focuses on an issue, anticipatory anxiety, that is unique to some fearful fliers. This group of people begins to worry days or weeks before a scheduled flight, sometimes so intensely they cannot sleep. Some readers who do not suffer from anticipatory anxiety may wish to skip chapter 8.

GETTING ADDITIONAL HELP: CAVEAT EMPTOR

Many people who enrolled in our seminars had invested thousands of dollars and dozens of hours with private practitioners without ridding themselves of their fear. If you decide to hire a mental health professional to assist, be an informed consumer. My recommendation is to avoid people who are offering fear-of-flying programs and services but are not properly licensed mental health professionals unless you believe that all you need is better, more accurate information. If you decide to see a mental health professional, I suggest that you choose one who uses a short-term cognitive behavioral approach. My opening statement with many of my clients was, "If we have not made substantial progress in five weeks, one of us is not doing their job." There are exceptions, notably people who suffer from agoraphobia or have other issues such as depression, but phobias are typically amenable to short-term treatment in my experience.

CHAPTER 2

Fears and Phobias

Professional counselors, psychologists, and social workers use a number of terms, including "anxiety," "fear," and "phobia" to describe human reactions. In this chapter, I will define some important concepts, particularly "fear" and "phobia," and discuss some others such as "worry," "anxiety," and "panic." In the final section of the chapter, I will briefly discuss the role of courage in overcoming fear. However, before I begin, I want to delve into the issue of how people acquire fears and phobias, beginning with the latter.

The following definitions were abstracted from the fourth edition of the *Diagnostic and Statistical Manual of Mental Disorders* (American Psychiatric Association 2000). This comprehensive manual is not widely available, but numerous online sources contain additional descriptive information for the curious (e.g., Factsheet: Phobias, found at www.nmha .org/go/phobias).

As mentioned, not everyone who hesitates to fly is aerophobic. People who suffer from *posttraumatic stress disorder* (PTSD) may be afraid to fly because they mistrust the "system," that is, everything from pilot training to the air traffic control system. People who suffer from *claustrophobia* (fear of enclosed spaces), *acrophobia* (fear of heights), and *agoraphobia* (fear of having a panic attack while unable to escape from the space where the panic attack is occurring) also avoid flying. A *phobia* is an irrational, intense, persistent fear of certain situations, activities, things, or persons. The main symptom of a phobia is the excessive, unreasonable desire to avoid the feared stimulus. When the fear is beyond one's control or if the fear interferes with daily life, a diagnosis of phobia is appropriate.

Fear is a response to an immediate dangerous situation, activity, thing, or person. By contrast, *anxiety* typically occurs without any external threat; it is internally generated. Anxiety is the result of perceived threats that are thought to be uncontrollable or unavoidable. *Worry* is one of the manifestations of anxiety.

There are several points worth highlighting in the foregoing definitions. First, fear is a rational, adaptive response. Human beings survived as a species because they could identify danger and either decide to flee from it or confront it. Phobias are irrational responses to nondangerous stimuli and may or may not be more intense than a normal response to a fear-inducing stimulus. For example, the response of a phobic flier is probably no more intense than that experienced by a California hiker who is suddenly confronted by a cougar on a mountain trail. Both phobias and fears evoke the fight-or-flight (no pun intended) mechanism, although the typical response of the person with a phobia is avoidance (flight).

Before they board the aircraft, fearful fliers often have thoughts (and thus anxiety) about crashes and dying. This is called *anticipatory anxiety*. After fearful fliers board the plane, the sights, sounds, and smells of the flight may stimulate fearful thoughts and, again, anxiety. However, if smoke begins to accumulate in the cabin during the flight, a fearful response is appropriate and prepares the passenger to deal with the situation.

Two other terms require definition: "panic" and "panic attack." Most dictionaries define *panic* as a sudden, overwhelming sense of terror. To this standard definition should be added that the person experiencing a *panic attack* has a sense of an impending catastrophe. It is not unusual for phobic fliers to panic and either decide not to board the plane or rush off the plane to avoid what they are sure is going to be a disaster. When fearful fliers panic, the source of the anxiety is internal images about what will occur if they stay on the plane. However, some people, particularly those suffering from agoraphobia, become anxious, not because they fear dying in a crash, but because they are afraid that they will have a panic attack and be unable to exit from the plane. They may also have mental images of panic-driven acts that will embarrass them or endanger others on the plane.

SOURCES OF FEARS AND PHOBIAS

Psychiatry in the United States has generally taken the position that most psychological maladies are the result of biological issues that result in an imbalance in enzymes, which in turn interrupt the normal functioning of the brain. This is not necessarily the perspective of many mental health professionals, psychiatrists in other countries, or every psychiatrist in the United States. Most mental health professionals agree that genetic factors probably predispose some people to the acquisition of phobias and other anxiety disorders.

Most human behavior, including irrational fear, is learned through various modeling processes. A behavior may be modeled by such variables as parent behavior, a television program, or a newspaper. Some of the fearful fliers that I have known had parents who were afraid to fly. It would be easy to conclude that genetics played a key role in the development of their disorder, but I also know many people who have parents and other relatives who are afraid to fly and have not developed the disorder. In this same vein, many fearful fliers' parents were not afraid to fly. What can we conclude from this information? The most likely explanation for the development of phobias is that both modeling and genetic factors play instrumental roles in the development of phobias.

But this is not the entire story. Many people become afraid to fly after "bad experiences" on an airplane in the absence of "good information." For example, turbulence is a normal part of flying, but many people do not understand that planes are built to withstand severe turbulence. After taking a turbulent flight, these fliers conclude that when the plane had encountered turbulent air, they had narrowly escaped death. Their thoughts that they had been about to die as a result of turbulence induced high anxiety during the flight. Once the plane landed, the anxiety dissipated rapidly and, by doing so, reinforced the belief. Put another way: an irrational fear was born because of a process known as *negative reinforcement*. Had these fliers known that, although turbulence is uncomfortable, it is not dangerous, the outcome might have been entirely different. Turbulence is scary, but accurate information can change your thoughts about it.

Genetics may predispose you to the development of irrational fears, but it is unlikely that a fear will erupt spontaneously because of your ancestors' genes. The fear of flying can be learned via modeling experiences regardless of the presence of predisposing genes. In light of this, I offer the following strategies to prevent the development of irrational fears among children and to prevent relapses among people who have overcome their fear.

Children and Prevention

Children under twelve years of age should not be allowed to watch or read about airline crashes. If they are exposed to news reports about crashes, they should receive a carefully worded explanation of what occurred and the facts about the safety of air travel.

Children who express fears about flying should not be belittled or otherwise made fun of by parents or others. Remember, fear is a normal response that is often the result of insufficient information. Give children the information they need to assess the risks associated with flying; encourage them to explore accurate sources of information. Finally, fearful fliers should refrain from any discussion or emotional demonstration of their fear when children who are less than twelve years of age are present. Even very young children are sensitive to the emotional reactions of their caretakers.

Recovering Fearful Fliers

People who are recovering from fear of flying should not read about or watch telecasts or webcasts that contain explicit information about, or photographic images of, air disasters, particularly in the period immediately following a crash (in the aftermath of an airplane crash, misinformation abounds about the cause of the accident).

When you decide to confront your fear, carefully investigate the options open to you. Treatment programs for phobias, except for agoraphobia, should be short (four to six sessions) and should involve practice flights, simulators, or virtual reality devices if at all possible. Treatment for other disorders, such as PTSD and agoraphobia with panic disorder, will take longer, but if your therapist or program director mentions years when discussing the duration of the treatment, run, do not walk, to the nearest exit. My firm belief is that a skilled therapist should be able to help most people who have specific phobias in ten sessions or less. The treatment for people with agoraphobia may also be of short duration, but often the treatment period is measured in months, not weeks.

If you are a recovering fearful flier, please avoid self-criticism related to your problem. Self-criticism lowers self-esteem and weakens your ability to muster the courage needed to confront the fear. You are not a "wimp" or a "wuss" because you are afraid of air travel. You are a judicious flier who wants all the facts before you get onto that beast that defies the laws of nature and flies—just kidding, sort of. Don't put yourself down!

When you decide to take your first flight after treatment has begun, do not schedule a flight that you may not be ready to take. For example, don't schedule your first flight from Los Angeles to Sydney, Australia, unless your fears are well controlled. Take a flight from Los Angeles to San Jose or a shuttle from New York City to Boston first and see how you do. After your effort to recover begins, take steps that will result in successes. Small accomplishments will build your self-confidence and pave the way to giant steps and great flights.

Do not plan flights that you are likely to avoid such as transcontinental or transoceanic flights. Start with short flights and work your way toward longer ones. One way to determine your readiness for a flight is by estimating the probability that you will actually take the flight. Use a 1–10 scale (with 1 being little or no confidence and 10 being complete confidence that you will take the flight). Avoidance worsens the fear and, if your confidence is low, the probability that you will avoid the flight is great. Similarly, do not book a flight if you doubt your ability to take the return flight. Not only will your anticipatory anxiety about the return trip ruin your business trip or vacation, but the usual result of not taking a return flight is either having to take an alternative means of transportation or forcing yourself onto an airliner while experiencing a high level of anxiety or by using alcohol or drugs to lower your anxiety level. The result is that the fear will become worse.

ISSUES OTHER THAN AEROPHOBIA

In the introduction to this chapter, I noted that several issues contribute to the fear of flying. In this section, claustrophobia, acrophobia, and other related issues will be addressed.

Claustrophobia

Claustrophobia is an intense fear of tight, enclosed spaces that a person erroneously believes may cause suffocation from lack of oxygen. Elevators are often a prime concern for people who suffer from claustrophobia, but airplanes are a close second. The passenger cabins on most airliners are long and narrow with low ceilings. To make matters worse, the cabins are often warm and stuffy. When cabin size, temperature, and poor ventilation while the plane is on the ground are taken together, it is easy to see why boarding a plane might induce a claustrophobic response. What happens? The person who suffers from claustrophobia expects to suffocate because of lack of oxygen, and the fear becomes a self-fulfilling prophecy: when that person boards the plane (or sometimes the jet bridge) he or she has difficulty breathing.

You probably just asked, "What is he talking about?" That's a good question. Typically we breathe diaphragmatically about twelve times per minute. The *diaphragm* is the large sheathlike muscle that sits under the rib cage and is operated by the autonomic nervous system. You breathe automatically and correctly until fear takes over. Fearful thoughts send the body into hyperdrive. Slow, *diaphragmatic breathing* is replaced by shallow, *thoracic breathing* (in the upper part of your chest) because the brain believes that the body needs to prepare for danger. The paradoxical aspect of this phenomenon is that too much oxygen is pumped into the bloodstream and the blood becomes deficient in carbon dioxide, with the result being that the claustrophobic feels as though he is not getting enough air. It gets worse. As the response continues, dizziness, blurred vision, and unconsciousness can occur. People with claustrophobia must learn to control their breathing and to know that airplanes are always filled with lots of air.

Acrophobia

Many people with acrophobia are not afraid to fly. Their fear is activated by high spaces where they feel vulnerable. A friend of mine will not stay in hotel rooms that are located on an upper floor. When his room is above the second floor, he insists on sleeping next to the inside wall. He is not afraid to fly, but I have encountered many people who perseverate on the mental image that somehow the floor of the plane will drop out and they will fall to the ground. After listening to a story much like this for more than an hour, I got out of my seat and commenced jumping up and down on the floor with the announced intention of having the floor drop out of the plane. After a minute or two, I invited the acrophobic flier to join me. He initially declined, but with the help of a caring flight attendant, he finally agreed. He learned that the floors on airplanes are quite substantial and can be trusted. That was my aim.

Posttraumatic Stress Disorder

As I said at the outset, there are many reasons that people avoid air travel, including posttraumatic stress disorder. Many people are probably familiar with PTSD because of the publicity given to soldiers returning from Iraq and Afghanistan who have developed the malady. PTSD occurs because individuals are exposed to stressful or traumatic events, such as war. One client developed PTSD after the side door to a B-747 United Airlines flight was ripped off in-flight and he saw nine passengers swept out of the plane. To make matters worse, it appeared that he would follow the nine through the 12 × 25–foot hole into a 22,000-foot free fall into the Pacific Ocean. It's understandable that he developed PTSD. However, PTSD may occur because of other types of traumatic experiences as well. Another client developed PTSD after one of his children was killed in a head-on accident in a mall parking lot after a shopping trip with her mother. A woman developed the disorder after she witnessed the death of her fiancé when the wheels from a large truck came loose and crushed his car.

People respond in different ways to traumatic experiences. A twenty-two-year-old Colombian woman was one of six survivors in a Central American airliner crash in which 120 passengers died. When she came to my seminar, her arms and hands were still bandaged to protect the skin grafts that were needed due to the burns she received as she scrambled out of the plane. She showed some signs of mild anxiety as we visited a stationary plane and discussed the graduation flight but no signs of PTSD. She took the graduation flight with her class and showed no reluctance to do so.

Children who have been sexually or physically abused, women who have been raped, victims of violent crimes of all types, and others who have been exposed to excessive levels of stress on their jobs may experience PTSD. Although people with PTSD exhibit a host of symptoms, the centerpiece for many is lack of trust. They do not trust the pilot ("He probably drinks"), the mechanics ("They don't have to do a good job because they are unionized"), or the air traffic controllers ("They are fatigued due to overwork"). Although all of these beliefs can be easily disputed, it is often the case that when one distrustful belief is confronted, another arises to take its place. All the erroneous beliefs must be replaced using valid sources of information that inspire trust along with techniques from cognitive behavioral therapy (CBT), which are the basis for the strategies outlined in this book.

Agoraphobia

Agoraphobic fearful fliers who have panic attacks and who are facing their fear of flying pose a serious challenge to mental health professionals. Earlier, a panic attack was defined as the sudden, intense onset of fear accompanied by thoughts of impending doom. How severe is the terror of a panic attack? I have had clients tell me that they would have welcomed a crash to end their fear. The first reaction of the person having a panic attack is to want to escape from the situation in which the attack is occurring. The obvious dilemma for a person experiencing a panic attack on an airplane is that she is trapped; there is no escape after the plane is airborne. Unfortunately, it is precisely this concern about the possibility of being trapped during a panic attack that then triggers the panic attack. In some instances, people who experience panic attacks also have some degree of social phobia and are afraid of doing something embarrassingly foolish in front of the crew and other passengers. For example, some fliers picture themselves clawing at and opening an exit in midflight to escape the intense emotion they are experiencing. If you are one of these people, forget it. There is no way that you will be able to open an exit door once the cabin is pressurized.

Passengers who have panic attacks may or may not be afraid that the plane will crash, but they often have many other obstacles to overcome if they are to become successful fliers. They must learn to travel to congested airports where they may get stuck in traffic (which can make them feel trapped), enter crowds of people (which can again activate their fear of being trapped as well as their social phobia), board a stuffy and crowded airplane, and be locked into a capsule from which there is no exit for the duration of the flight. That is a tall order, but it can be done. Let me reword that: it must be done, at least to the point that the person is able to leave home and travel around the city. Agoraphobia often worsens with neglect, particularly if an individual abandons efforts to leave a safe place. You can have a great life without ever flying. The same cannot be said if you are so fearful that you cannot leave home.

COURAGE

I have mentioned 9/11 frequently and I will continue to do so. It is a point in time that none of us will ever forget. I watched as the airplanes crashed into the twin towers of the World Trade Center. I also watched the firefighters and police officers respond heroically to a very grave situation. They and the passengers aboard the United Airlines flight that crashed near Shanksville, Pennsylvania, faced the very real possibility that they would perish. If you have an intense fear of flying, you will need the same type of courage to address your fear that those men and women demonstrated on that fateful day.

CHAPTER 3

The Physiology of Fear

When you have a fearful thought, your brain sends a signal to your hypothalamus gland to mobilize your body for action. The hypothalamus gland regulates your autonomic nervous system and controls such bodily functions as your heartbeat and breathing. Let me illustrate what happens with a personal example. Recently, I was walking in the woods near my home when I had a very close encounter with a poisonous copperhead snake. My immediate response was to jump away from the snake to avoid the danger I perceived. The elapsed time between when I saw the snake and my reaction to it would have to be measured in tenths or hundredths of a second. While my response probably did not save my life, because copperhead bites are rarely fatal, it did save me a great deal of pain. You have probably had similar responses to danger, perhaps as you were driving on the freeway and the automobile or truck beside you suddenly swerved into your lane. Your response: Get out of harm's way. That response may have saved your life, and this same response has saved countless millions of people's lives over the history of humankind.

The response to danger described here is called the *fight-or-flight response*. All animals have it; it is a normal and necessary part of human existence and has allowed us to continue to thrive as a species. However, the fight-or-flight response occurs in relation to perceived danger, whether the danger is real or imagined. When the danger is real, the fight-or-flight response is useful. When the response is to an exaggerated danger (a phobic response), it must be controlled.

The first step in controlling your physiological response to perceived danger of flying is to understand what happens to your body. But before I begin the discussion of your automatic response to fearful thoughts, I want to address the idea of the controllability of these responses. Our heart beats and we breathe without conscious effort, that is, we do not have to cognitively remind our heart to beat or our breathing mechanism to work so that we will have enough air. They work automatically. I am often asked the question, "If all of this occurs automatically, how can I influence the processes?" You can influence these automatic responses by putting your conscious mind into override mode: to be successful, you must learn how the automatic responses occur and then use strategies that mental health professionals have used for decades to help people control their bodies.

THE RELATIONSHIP BETWEEN THOUGHTS AND PHYSICAL RESPONSES

The beginning point of the fight-or-flight reaction is your thoughts. This idea is very hard for some people to accept because of the short elapsed time between the perception that danger is at hand and the response to it. It may be useful to recall that scary thoughts about flying occur automatically, and any thoughts about flying will evoke scary thoughts to some degree. For example, some fearful fliers who participated in our seminars won their companies' sales contests only to learn that their rewards were all-expenses-paid trips to destinations such as Hawaii. The thought of flying to these destinations activated their fear. Imagine that you are driving by the airport on your way to work and you look out your automobile window and see a plane take off. What would your reaction be? Can you feel your body begin to respond to the danger? Have you ever agreed to take a friend to the airport and, as you approached the airport, remembered your last flying experience and started to get sweaty palms? Thoughts about flying, enclosed spaces, and being high above the ground can initiate the physiological responses needed to fight or flee. When you change your thoughts about the things that scare you, this troublesome response will no longer occur.

Fearful Thoughts: Before the Flight

Some people start having thoughts about crashing and dying days, weeks, and even months prior to their actual flights. These people may become forgetful or lose focus from time to time. One participant wrecked his automobile because of a "premonition" regarding his flight. Chapter 8 will be devoted to eliminating this response. Unless you learn to control your fear of fear—your anticipatory anxiety—the likelihood that you will stop flying is substantial because the psychological pain of the anxiety becomes too great to bear.

Physical Responses to Flying: An In-Depth Look

Let's take an in-depth look at what happens to your body when you have an intense, fearful thought. As you now know, this thought activates your body to respond to a perceived danger—flying. The moment the thought occurs, epinephrine is pumped into the bloodstream and several physiological events occur simultaneously. These changes are described in the following sections.

CARDIOVASCULAR CHANGES

Blood vessels constrict, blood pressure goes up, and the rate at which your heart beats increases dramatically, often going from a resting rate of 72 beats per minute to over 140 beats a minute. Also, the blood flows from your hands, feet, and brain to your central body cavity. Additionally, the composition of the blood changes because blood sugar increases. Blood sugar is pumped into the blood to fuel the physical reaction to the danger. The combined reactions of the cardiovascular system produce a symptom that actually adds to and increases the fear for many fliers: because their hearts are beating so rapidly and seem to be out of control, many fear that they will have a heart attack.

A less alarming result of the changes in the cardiovascular system is sweaty palms. The fact that palms start to sweat is paradoxical because the hands and feet actually get colder during the fight-or-flight reaction. However, because the capillaries function differently in the mobilized state caused by a high level of epinephrine in the system, the palms do sweat, sometimes profusely.

Finally, some fearful fliers who suffer from a condition called *mitral valve prolapse* (MVP) may find that it is worsened by the intense fight-or-flight response. MVP is a heart condition that is usually harmless. It is a problem that occurs mostly in women and is a mechanical abnormality that causes irregular heartbeat and heart palpitations. Both of these symptoms can and often do accelerate when people are experiencing stress. If you suffer from MVP and have not consulted with your physician, please do so as soon as possible. Unless the consultation assures you that the palpitations you have while you are flying are not a threat to your health, my advice is to stay off of airplanes.

RESPIRATORY SYSTEM

As noted earlier, your breathing also changes quite dramatically when you have intense, fearful thoughts. Because your body requires more oxygen to fight or flee from the perceived danger, your breathing rate increases from its normal rate (six to fifteen breaths per minute) to twenty, thirty, or more breaths per minute. Not only does the rate change, but, as described in chapter 2, the manner in which you breathe changes: you breathe thoracically rather than diaphragmatically. Thoracic breathing quickly enriches your blood with oxygen and discards (via exhalation) carbon dioxide.

You can become aware of how you are breathing by placing your hand on your stomach just below your rib cage and breathing normally. If you are breathing diaphragmatically, your hand will rise as you inhale and fall when you exhale. Why is this? As your lungs fill during the inhale in the normal breathing process, they expand. As they expand, they apply pressure to your stomach, which moves outward to make room for the enlarging lungs. Just the opposite reaction occurs as you exhale, letting the air out of your lungs. Pay attention to your own breathing process for a few moments to familiarize yourself with it. This knowledge is an essential first step toward taking control of the fight-or-flight reaction.

Now place one hand on your stomach, the other hand on your upper chest, and tense your abdominal muscles (those just over your stomach) to get a sense of what happens when you breathe thoracically. Once you tense your stomach muscles, almost all movement will cease in the lower part of your abdomen and the hand placed on your upper chest will begin to move. Also, you will probably note that your breathing rate increases if you continue to tense your abdominal muscles. The change in breathing that occurs when you breathe thoracically results in blood that becomes oxygen rich and also carbon dioxide deficient, particularly when there is no physical activity to burn up the extra oxygen.

THE BRAIN

Because of several factors—the fear, the presence of epinephrine, and the fact that some of the blood that is normally found in the cranial cavity surrounding the brain has been pumped into that part of the body that houses the vital organs such as the heart—the brain functions quite differently when you experience the fight-or-flight response. The brain actually shifts to what can best be termed a survival mode and operates from a very primitive part called the *brain stem*. Fearful fliers often report that before and during flights they cannot "think." This is actually a fairly accurate representation of what occurs. When you are intensely afraid, you are almost completely cut off from accessing information stored in the cerebrum, even if it was recently stored there. Many fearful fliers cannot remember what clothes they packed for the trip, are unable to find their car keys when they are ready to go to the airport, and are totally unable to perform even the most basic cognitive tasks, such as reading, let alone higher-level tasks, such as preparing for a business meeting.

Finally, because of the shortage of carbon dioxide that results from the change in breathing, certain portions of the brain induce dizziness. If the shortage of carbon dioxide is severe and prolonged, you will pass out, which is the body's way of taking over the breathing process and restoring the appropriate oxygen–carbon dioxide balance. Please remember that if you get dizzy and pass out, it is because you are experiencing a shortage of carbon dioxide, not because of a deficit of oxygen, as most people believe. This shortage of carbon dioxide also produces one of the scariest symptoms associated with the fear of flying, a choking sensation that seems very much like suffocation. This is particularly disconcerting for people who suffer from claustrophobia because they expect to experience a lack of air in enclosed spaces. In chapter 4, you will learn how to recognize this response and cope with it.

MUSCLES

Muscles tense in response to perceived fear. If the period of fear is short in duration, the tension will dissipate quite quickly. However, if you have anticipatory anxiety and then take a long plane trip, muscle tension can produce a great deal of discomfort and even severe pain. The *temporomandibular joint* (TMJ, which is located at the point where the lower jaw is fastened to the skull), the *trapezius muscles* (which are located on top of the shoulders), the muscles in the lower back, and the muscles in the calves and legs seem most problematic in this regard. One of the most common sights in our seminars for fearful fliers was participants rubbing their backs and the tops of their shoulders by noon on the first day. If you find yourself massaging your trapezius muscles, suffering from lower back pain, or tapping your feet, the muscle tension has reached the point where you need to take charge of it.

Muscle tension produces some symptoms other than tension and pain. One of these is uncontrollable shaking, particularly of the legs. Some fearful fliers are so embarrassed by this that they carry jackets to place over their legs so others will not notice the movement. Another symptom that results from a combination of factors, including muscle tension, is that the legs seem too weak to provide the needed support. Some fearful fliers will not get out of their seats because they are afraid that they will collapse in the aisle. This will not happen!

Finally, as muscle tension builds, some fearful fliers become so distraught that they fear they will attack a flight attendant or literally throw open the emergency exits while the plane is in flight. As far as I know, a fearful flier has never attacked a flight attendant, or anyone else on an airplane, and don't worry about opening the emergency exits while you are in flight: it is impossible for you to open the plug-type doors and windows that make up the safety exits. As the plane is pressurized, the air pressure on the exit doors increases to the point that an entire professional football team pulling simultaneously with all their strength would be unable to open one. It was the case that at one time some planes were equipped with rear exits that could be opened in flight. In 1972 a bank robber forced a flight attendant to open one of these exits in flight and then parachuted from the plane. Soon afterward these exits were equipped with external locks that close automatically once the plane is airborne.

VISION

A few fearful fliers experience blurred vision, primarily because too much oxygen in the bloodstream causes the pupils of the eyes to dilate. One person reported that this problem persisted after the flight, probably because she had "flashbacks" that created intense physical reactions. Paradoxically, at the outset of the fight-or-flight reaction, your vision can be somewhat improved because of your heightened physical state.

HEARING

One reaction to your fear is that your hearing improves. This, and your heightened physical and psychological states, means that you can hear the mechanical sounds of the aircraft much better than people who are not afraid. Many fearful fliers report asking the person sitting next to them if they had heard a sound that they were certain was an engine exploding, only to learn that the other person had heard nothing.

GASTROINTESTINAL REACTIONS

Your stomach may become upset because, as a reaction to your fear, the lining of your stomach secretes more acid. Additionally, when you breathe rapidly and shallowly, you can draw more air into your stomach, a condition not unlike what occurs when young babies cry. When these two conditions occur, together or separately, they can upset your stomach. Lower gastrointestinal distress can also occur in the form of diarrhea.

MEDICATION, ALCOHOL, AND THE REACTION TO FEAR

Many people at our seminars for fearful fliers came grasping a variety of medications, including Valium (diazepam), Xanax (alprazolam), Klonopin (clonazepam), and Ativan (lorazepam), all of which are anti-anxiety medications. One person came "equipped" with ten small bottles of vodka. Some of the people who came with the medication had not taken it before but in their preparation for the seminar had visited their physicians, who had prescribed some form of medication. Others had taken medication before, but once they were in the seminar learned that it did not produce the results they desired. Many of our enrollees had used (and abused) alcohol to help them fly, including some who were nondrinkers except when they flew. In a few instances, the abuse of alcohol had been so great that people had become alcoholics. When these people came to terms with their drinking problem and stopped drinking, they no longer had the crutch that had allowed them to fly.

I am not against the use of antianxiety medication as one tool to help you overcome your fear of flying, with one exception, which I will discuss in the next paragraph. I am against the use of medication and alcohol as the *sole* tool in your effort to deal with your fear. Why is this? First, neither alcohol nor antianxiety medications are curative, which means that you will have to rely on them for the rest of your life if they are your only weapons against fear. Second, if you are intensely afraid, medication and alcohol will be of no use to you unless you are prepared to take them in large doses and actually knock yourself out, which should never be done. Third, alcohol and the medications listed earlier are addictive. An addiction to some of the medications can develop in as little as a week of continuous use for drugs like Xanax (alprazolam). Moreover, once you become addicted to Xanax and some of the other drugs listed previously, it takes at least thirty days for the withdrawal to occur as you gradually wean yourself from them. It upsets me greatly that many physicians fail to share information about the addictiveness of these medications with their patients.

As I mentioned, there is one exception to my endorsement of the use of antianxiety medications to overcome the fear of flying. Some fearful fliers are prone to addiction, that is, they have personalities susceptible to addiction. If you have ever been addicted to drugs or alcohol, my best advice is to avoid the use of drugs as a part of your treatment. Drugs may make the flying process a bit easier, but you run the risk of trading one problem (the fear of flying) for another (an addiction to drugs).

How does the body react to drugs and alcohol when you are afraid? Let me hedge on the answer to this question by saying that it depends entirely upon the intensity of your fear, your weight, and your physical condition. My advice is simple: never use excessive amounts of either drugs or alcohol to combat your fear. Moreover, mixing alcohol and drugs increases your risk of injury or death. I have heard reports of people with mild, sporadic fear who were much more comfortable after one drink or one 0.25 milligram Xanax pill. However, these reports seem to be the exceptions. One fearful flier reported drinking a dozen bourbon and Cokes in two hours with no lessening of her fear. Another flier reported that he took six 0.25 milligram Xanax and drank seven Scotch and waters in three hours yet experienced no reduction in his physical or cognitive response. Many other people report taking large amounts of pills and alcohol with no noticeable impact on their fear until they land. One fearful flier regularly stepped off the flight, threw up, and became immediately drunk. Many others, who flew for business purposes, arrived a day early for their meetings so they could recover from the pills and booze they had absorbed on their trips.

Recall that all of the physical reactions to the fear begin with the perception of being in danger. These thoughts produce the physical responses described previously, responses that have developed over the course of our evolution to allow us to cope with danger. What happens when you take an antianxiety medication or drink an alcoholic drink when you are afraid? The immediate response is relaxation, because alcohol and antianxiety medications depress heart rate, slow breathing, and so on. The brain, stimulated by the continuing fear, senses that your body is no longer ready to deal with the danger (that it has relaxed) and pumps more epinephrine into your bloodstream, which in turn stimulates the heart, tenses the muscles, and alters your breathing. If you take another pill or absorb another drink, the brain increases the level of epinephrine in your bloodstream again, and so it goes until the alcohol or medication level in your bloodstream is so overpowering that you pass out or are numb.

I have observed a small number of fearful fliers, including my wife, Sandra, who is now a recovered fearful flier, try to douse their fears with alcohol. They were unsuccessful. I also observed two fearful fliers who were enrolled in our seminars rely on the pills their doctors had prescribed to medicate themselves into a slobbering oblivion rather than rely on the strategies we taught them. They boarded the plane, but it was a small victory. In my view, the twin risks of addiction and failure to conquer your fear are too great to allow either physician-prescribed medication or "self-medication" with alcohol to serve as your primary defense against the fear of flying.

IDENTIFYING YOUR SYMPTOMS

In chapter 4, you will be given strategies to control all of your thoughts as well as your physical reactions to your fear. After you have developed a valid information base about flying, you will be given techniques in chapter 8 for dealing with anticipatory anxiety. However, to take advantage of the material in these chapters, you must identify your physical reactions to fear. Table 1 is a checklist of symptoms experienced by fearful fliers. Please go through this list carefully and then identify and place a check next to the symptoms you experience as a result of your fear.

The numbers in the right-hand column correspond to strategies for controlling the symptoms listed; these strategies are included at the end of table 1.

Table 1: Symptoms Produced by the Fear of Flying		
Cognitive Symptoms		**Strategies**
☐	Racing, irrational thoughts	1, 8
☐	Forgetfulness—short-term memory loss	1
☐	Dizziness	2
☐	Out-of-body experience: feeling of observing oneself	2
☐	Passing out	2
☐	Concentration impossible	1, 2
☐	Cannot speak coherently	1, 2
Cardiovascular Symptoms		**Strategies**
☐	Racing heart	2, 3
☐	Palpitations/irregular heartbeat (MVP)	5, 6

Respiratory Symptoms	Strategies
☐ Tightness in throat and chest	2
☐ Rapid breathing/panting	2
☐ Cannot get a full breath	2
Vision Symptoms	**Strategies**
☐ Blurred vision	2
Hearing Symptoms	**Strategies**
☐ Fear heightened by mechanical sounds	2
Muscle Symptoms	**Strategies**
☐ Discomfort in the TMJ, trapezius, or other muscles	4
☐ Legs shaking uncontrollably	4
☐ Feeling uncoordinated	4
☐ Urge to hit someone or "tear open" the exits	1, 2, 4
☐ Biting nails, tapping foot, or other nervous habit	2, 4
Stomach/Intestine Symptoms	**Strategies**
☐ Butterflies, queasiness	2
☐ Eating all the time or not at all	2, 4, 7
☐ Vomiting	1, 2, 6
☐ Diarrhea	1, 2, 6
Other Symptoms	**Strategies**
☐ Hands and feet getting cold	2
☐ Face flushing	2
☐ Palms perspiring	2
☐ Tingling or numbness in hands, lips, or other parts	2

Strategy Key	
1. Stop racing thoughts (rubber band and injunction).	5. Check with physician.
2. Control breathing.	6. Medicate if necessary.
3. Use Valsalva maneuver.	7. Eliminate related concerns.
4. Relax muscles with ITR.	8. Secure valid information.

Most of the strategies and the symptoms they control are discussed in detail in chapter 4, and chapters 5–7 contain the facts you need to develop a valid information base about flying. Briefly, racing, irrational thoughts can be controlled by a combination of thought stopping (1) and developing a valid information base (8) about flying. For example, you must understand why planes are able to fly, that the air traffic control system is safe, and that generally you are much more likely to die in your automobile or a taxi as you drive across town than in an airplane. A (2) opposite the symptom indicates that it can be controlled by breathing techniques designed to return your breathing to normal. A racing heart can be slowed by either controlling your breathing (2) or by using the Valsalva maneuver (3). Actually, there are several strategies that can be employed to slow a racing heart, and you will need to learn one if you are concerned about this problem.

Some symptoms can be controlled by the use of deep muscle relaxation strategies (4). If you have mitral valve prolapse, you should see a physician (5) and you may require medication (6). Because some problems develop as a result of anticipatory anxiety, they can only be dealt with by eliminating or reducing this part of your problem (7). The details will be covered later, but the important point for you to hear at this time is that all of your symptoms can be controlled. It is up to you to learn how to control them.

BACK TO THOUGHTS

The symptoms listed in table 1 are the result of catastrophic thoughts about flying. Unfortunately, the symptoms also give rise to other scary thoughts that heighten the fear: it is a vicious cycle that must be broken.

I have already noted that a rapid heartbeat causes some fearful fliers to think they will have a heart attack. Tightness in the throat and chest can cue thoughts about suffocation, just as mechanical sounds can initiate thoughts of falling and crashes. The physical symptoms resulting from fear are bad enough to endure in and of themselves, but sometimes the thoughts they spawn are unbearable.

However, there is some good news in all of this. One of the obvious ways in which the entire process can be halted is by stopping the catastrophic thoughts. Another way to gain control of your fear is to eliminate or control the physical symptoms produced by those scary thoughts. The ability to slow your heart rate, control your breathing, and reduce your muscle tension will restore your belief that you are in control of your body, which can be tremendously empowering. Though your goal should be to replace catastrophic thoughts with rational beliefs about flying, know that you can control the physical symptoms even if your mind races. I have seen people who could not shut down their minds but who were able to take control of their bodies. Ultimately, to rid yourself of this fear, you must learn to control both your thoughts and your physical responses, but learning to do one is not necessarily linked to the other. This is very important for you to know if you are one of the fearful fliers who, most of all, hates the physical symptoms you experience when you fly.

CHAPTER 4

Techniques for Coping with Fearful Responses

What is curative? How can you rid yourself of this despicable problem that interferes with your life? You can start to do this by compiling an accurate database about flying to replace your current beliefs (chapters 5–7), by eliminating your anticipatory anxiety (chapter 8), and by coping with your fear on the plane (chapter 9). Once you learn that you can control your thoughts, muscle tension, heart rate, and breathing, planes will be less frightening. If you can recall the information presented in chapters 5–7 while cruising at 35,000 feet or when the plane is in turbulence, your fear will either be gone or minimized to the point that you will have only one thought: "I can fly."

To reach the point of being able to control your thoughts, you must first learn the techniques discussed in this chapter. As a first step, you must learn to "measure" your fear to ascertain whether you are making progress.

MEASURING YOUR FEAR

You can measure your fear using what Joseph Wolpe (1969) called a *SUDS* (subjective units of disturbance scale). This is a *subjective scale* because it is your measure of your fear rather than a *normative scale*, where you would compare your fear response to the responses of other people.

I want you to begin to learn to measure your fear by thinking about a time when you are perfectly relaxed. For some people this is the time just prior to dropping off to sleep. For others it is when they are lying on the beach listening to the sounds of the surf and sea birds. That place of perfect relaxation is a 1 on your subjective scale. Now think about a time when you are most scared, when your fear is at its highest level. This represents a 10 on your SUDS scale and means that you are intensely afraid, as scared as you can get. Your SUDS score may never have been up to 10 on an airplane, but if you have the active imagination most fearful fliers have, you can imagine yourself at this point. A 5 on your SUDS scale is the halfway point between being perfectly relaxed and totally frightened. Now estimate the extent of your fear for each of the following segments of the flight using the SUDS scores (1–10) just described.

Going to airport   _____

Taxiing   _____

Taking off   _____

Cruising   _____

Descending   _____

Landing   _____

As you work on conquering your fear, continue to use your SUDS score to measure the intensity of your fear. You will also be using your SUDS score as a partial basis for establishing goals for your graduation flight (a process to be described in chapter 10). Finally, and most importantly, you will be using your SUDS score to determine whether the techniques described in the subsequent sections of this chapter actually work.

STOPPING RACING THOUGHTS

Fearful fliers know that once the fear develops, the catastrophic thoughts about flying come automatically. The thoughts seem to be premonitions about your flight, but they are not. Almost everyone who took our fear-of-flying seminars had the premonition that the headline in the local newspaper would read, "Fearful Flier Class Members Die in Fiery

Crash!" Others had thoughts about having panic attacks, embarrassing themselves in the plane, or suffocating in that cramped airplane cabin.

Perhaps the worst thoughts are those that begin when the door is about to be closed: "I'll be trapped with no place to go for the next two hours," "I'll die and never see my children again!" "We'll hit turbulence and the plane will spiral out of control and we'll all die!" and so on. All of these thoughts must be stopped, but how?

These thoughts are automatic and ignoring them will not work. Instead, you must take direct, assertive action to deal with the fearful thoughts that enter your mind. *Thought stopping* is a simple but effective technique that involves five steps:

1. Identify the scary thought and *decide* that you do not want it anymore.

2. Snap yourself in the palm of your hand with a sturdy rubber band. This will hurt!

3. Tell yourself, usually in your native language, to *stop* thinking those thoughts.

4. Remind yourself, "I can handle my fear."

5. Repeat these four steps as often as necessary.

Step 1

The thoughts that come to you about flying are, for the most part, irrational, which means they are exaggerations of the things that are likely to occur on airplanes. The reason they scare you is that you believe the false message (FEAR, which is "False Evidence Appearing Real"). You need to reframe FEAR to mean "Forget Everything and Recover." To do this, you must recognize the irrational thought and actively decide that you want to dismiss it, in effect saying, "I choose to dismiss you."

Step 2

On the day of the flight, you need to place a rubber band around your hand so that it is positioned just over your palm. Choose a thick rubber band that fits snugly over your hand but does not cut off the circulation. The rubber band should be thick for two reasons. First, it will be sturdier and thus it will not break with repeated use. (Yes, you may have to use it several times!) Second, believe it or not, the thicker rubber bands do not sting as much as the thin ones. I tested this "theory" one day in a large office-supply store. I proceeded to snap the palms of my hands with various types of rubber bands while several people looked at me as though I had gone over the edge. What happens when you snap yourself with a rubber band? It hurts! It stings! More importantly, it interrupts the racing thoughts that drive you off of or make you uncomfortable on planes.

Step 3

The next step in the process is to issue an injunction to yourself to stop thinking those irrational thoughts. This order to yourself should be sharp and decisive, and if you can muster it, accompanied by anger directed at your fear, never at yourself. This order to "Stop!" should come from your own self-talk, and for most people, should be in their first language ("*Basta!*" in Spanish, for example). The one exception that I have encountered is French. Some of the French-speaking participants in our seminars indicated that it simply takes too long to yell "Stop!" in French. I do not speak French and thus did not argue the point at the time. However, a mental, nonvocal "Quit!" in English might serve as the needed reminder. Think for a moment how you talk to yourself. Are there single words or brief phrases that you use to stop thought patterns in your nonflying life? If there are, these might be effective in stopping your irrational thoughts about flying. Do you swear in your self-talk? Some people find it easier to conjure up anger at their fear if they swear at it. Your injunction should be brief and decisive. Furthermore, it should not contain a personal "put-down" such as "Stop, Stupid." Remember, you weaken your ability to cope with your fear when you engage in self-criticism.

If you cannot come up with an injunction of your own, try some of the following ones that have been used very successfully by people like you:

- "Stop this s---."

- Deborah (in her mother's voice): "Stop!"

- "In your face."

- "No more."

- "Enough already!"

- "Cut the crap."

- "Quit."

- "Damn you!"

Generating anger to accompany the injunction is difficult for many people. This is partly because they cannot imagine themselves being aggressive with their fear because it seems so powerful. Also, some people never permit themselves to feel anger for any reason. As a means of getting in touch with your anger, it may be useful for you to make a list of the costs that have been associated with your fear. What has your fear cost you in terms of money—lost jobs, cancelled flights, and lost opportunities to make money, such as taking a promotion? What has it cost you in terms of relationships—missed family reunions, graduations, baptisms, and bar mitzvahs? What has it cost you in terms of fun—missed vacations and missed opportunities to be with friends and family? The costs associated with the fear of flying are often astronomical when put in terms of money, relationships, and fun. Finally, it is okay to feel anger, particularly if it is for a good cause. What better cause could there be than defeating your fear of flying?

A SWAT team member of a large metropolitan police force had always called himself terrible names because he was afraid to fly. He had vivid memories of his panic attacks, which he was sure would reoccur if he flew. When he switched his focus and called his fear names rather than demeaning himself, he turned the corner and began to fly. You can too!

Step 4

"I can" or power statements should follow the injunction to stop. When you tell yourself that you *can* do something, you are affirming that you have the techniques and personal strength needed to do it. In the case of flying, you are telling yourself that you can handle your fear and fly. Self-affirming positive statements, like injunctions, need to be brief and to the point. To develop your positive self-statements, you may need to review your strengths. Identify any adversity that you have overcome and any triumphs in your personal or career world, and then develop a statement such as those developed by triumphant fearful fliers before you. One woman related that she had climbed to the top of a male-dominated organization over untold opposition. She said, "I know what they say about me behind my back—'She's one tough bitch'—and they are right." That phrase, as distasteful as it might be to some, became a part of her master plan to overcome another obstacle: fear of flying. Some of the following positive self-statements may help you write your own:

- "I can handle this!"
- Try visualizing this: "I can!!!"
- "I've done harder things."
- "I'm stronger than my fear."
- "My fear can't stop me."
- "I can defeat my fear."

Some people cannot imagine themselves being strong and thus cannot come up with statements affirming their personal power. If you are one of these people, replace the affirming self-statement with a motivational statement. This motivational statement should reflect your reason for wanting to overcome your fear. One woman, who had never flown, wanted to join her husband in Paris to celebrate their thirtieth wedding anniversary. Her motivational statement was, "I'll see Paris when I conquer my fear." My favorite motivational statement comes from dozens of people who had conquered many fears but were still hampered by their fear of flying. They often used the statement, "When I fly, I'll be free!"

Barriers to Using Thought Stopping

There are three major barriers that you must overcome if you are to use thought stopping successfully. The first barrier is that it is painful, and many people in our seminars said, "I'm not into pain." But you are if you tolerate your fear of flying. Think of all the psychological pain you have endured because of your fear. You have certainly been scared, which is painful. You may have been humiliated when you got off a plane at the last moment. Is that not painful? What about the loneliness you have experienced because you missed a vacation, wedding, or family get-together? The momentary physical pain you will experience as a result of snapping yourself with a rubber band is nothing compared to the psychological pain that you have already endured.

The second barrier is the embarrassment that some people feel when they snap themselves because they are concerned that other people may notice and think that they are weird. These people are typically what I have referred to as "cool fearful fliers," which means they give no external sign of being afraid, even when they are terrified. Recall that I stood in an office-supply store and snapped myself with numerous rubber bands while more than one person gave me an inquisitive look. It was a bit embarrassing. However, you must be able to do two things in order to get over your embarrassment. The first of these is to give yourself permission to take some risks while you are recovering from your fear. Taking risks means doing some things that are out of the ordinary for you. The second thing is to use your sense of humor. One fearful flier, who was riding in first class, told a seat mate that the rubber band he was wearing was a Rolex accessory, a story made somewhat credible by the presence of a $20,000 Rolex on his left wrist. Another flier related that her color-coordinated rubber band was a new European fashion accessory. Never mind that she bought it at the supermarket, and that if you turned it over it read "Fly Crazy." However, my best advice is that if you snap the rubber band and your seat mate looks at you inquisitively or judgmentally, lean over and whisper, "If I don't snap this thing once in a while, I throw up." I can personally guarantee that the person sitting next to you will be delighted to have you snap your rubber band.

The third barrier is the superstitious belief that thinking irrational thoughts keeps the plane in the air. It is true that, if you have flown in the past, you worried and the plane arrived safely. You may even have "helped" by listening to every sound, counting the screws on the wings to see if any were missing, watching the faces of the flight attendants for any sign of panic, looking out the window for other planes that might be on a collision course with your plane, and so forth. Unfortunately, your hypervigilant behavior became linked to the safe arrival of the plane.

Giving up your superstitious belief that your monitoring actually was the factor that ensured the safety of the flight may be more scary than flying itself. I can only assure you that you had nothing to do with the plane arriving safely. It is impossible for a relatively small person sitting inside the plane to hold up a modern jetliner that may weigh from 100,000 to 1,000,000 pounds. The air traffic control system and the onboard Traffic Alert and Collision Avoidance System (TCAS) keep the planes a safe distance apart, not your watchful behavior. Decide now to give up these irrational thoughts.

CONTROLLING YOUR BREATHING

As you now know, when you have scary thoughts, your brain prepares your body to do battle by pumping epinephrine into your bloodstream. One of the immediate changes is that your breathing becomes faster and shallower. This throws off carbon dioxide and pumps more oxygen into your bloodstream. The result is that you may feel a choking sensation in your throat and become light-headed. This process is 100 percent controllable, and you must control it in order to restore both your body's and brain's functioning to normal. You should begin to control your breathing the moment you recognize the scary thought, snap your rubber band, tell yourself to *stop* thinking those thoughts, and affirm that you can handle your fear.

There are many techniques that can be used to control breathing. The one I am recommending, I call the RED technique because it will control the Rate, Exhale, and Diaphragm. Your goals should be to breathe less than twenty times per minute, to control the exhale so that you always breathe out very slowly, and to fill your lungs from the bottom using the diaphragm. But how do you do this? Here's the technique:

1. *Inhale.* The moment that you snap your rubber band, begin to inhale, forcing yourself to breathe from your diaphragm and thus fill your lungs from the bottom. It may help to place your hand on your stomach just below the rib cage and push in when you inhale to remind yourself to force the diaphragm to work. Time your inhale. Count: one thousand one, one thousand two, one thousand three.

2. *Hold your breath.* At the count of one thousand three, hold your breath. As you hold your breath, count again: one thousand one, one thousand two, one thousand three.

3. *Purse your lips and exhale.* At this point, purse your lips as though you are going to kiss your sister and begin to exhale through your lips, again counting: one thousand one, one thousand two, one thousand three.

4. *Rest without inhaling or exhaling.* Now comes the hard part. After you have expelled the air from your lungs on the exhale, rest, neither inhaling or exhaling. As you do, count: one thousand one, one thousand two, one thousand three.

5. *Repeat.* Once you reach one thousand three, you are ready to begin the process all over again with your next inhalation. Repeat the process for five to seven minutes.

If the process of controlling your breathing sounds easy, it is, except for two points in the process. When you manually take over the breathing process, you will find that you want to inhale very quickly because your brain is telling you that you are suffocating. It is lying to you, and you must remind yourself that you actually have a *shortage* of carbon dioxide and an *oversupply* of oxygen. The second difficult point will be when you are supposed to rest at the end of the first cycle. Because it takes a few minutes for the symptoms associated with hyperventilation to subside, your brain will say you are still suffocating. Don't believe it!

It may help you to combat the fear of suffocation to remind yourself that the worst thing that can occur if you hyperventilate is that you will pass out. If that were to happen, your body would take over, you would breathe normally, and the oxygen–carbon dioxide balance would be restored. You would then wake up, and though you might be a little embarrassed, you would be fine.

The RED technique slows your breathing to a rate of twelve to fifteen times a minute, forces you to control the exhale, and employs the diaphragm in the breathing process. In five to seven minutes, much of your body's functioning will be restored to normal, including your heart rate and the temperature of your hands. You will also find that you can get in touch with the rational part of your brain, and, if you have acquired the knowledge you need to offset your misinformation about flying, you can combat your scary thoughts using accurate information.

A Caveat

I have seen hundreds of people use the RED technique to control their bodily responses to fear while they were flying. A few of these people reported difficulty in totally eliminating the light-headed feeling. Typically, this happens because the muscles involved in breathing have not become totally relaxed. There are three sets of muscles involved in breathing that can become so tense that they interfere with normal breathing: the muscles in the chest, the diaphragm, and, for some people, the throat muscles. If you are using the RED technique and you remain light-headed, relax these muscles, and the dizziness will dissipate:

1. First, concentrate on the muscles in the chest.

    a. Square your shoulders and lift your hands into a fighting position. Do not clench your fists!

    b. Now, within the confines of a coach-class seating area (use a dining room chair for practice), try to touch your elbows behind your back. When you have forced your elbows as far toward each other as you can, hold the tension that develops in the chest muscles and count: one thousand one, one thousand two, one thousand three. Place your hands in your lap and simultaneously tell yourself, "Relax," and release the tension by moving your hands toward each other. Let the tension flow from your chest as you relax.

    c. Repeat three to five times or until the muscles in the chest area are relaxed.

2. Next relax the diaphragm. This will be difficult and will cause some discomfort.

    a. Imagine that you are about to suck the skin of your abdomen under your rib cage using only your stomach muscles. Now begin to suck your stomach *in* and *up* under your ribs. This will be difficult. When you have pulled as much of your skin in and up as possible, hold the tension and count: one thousand one, one thousand two, one thousand three, one thousand four, one thousand five. Release the tension and tell yourself, "Relax," and let the tension flow from the stomach.

    b.   Repeat until light-headedness dissipates.

3.   For a few people, the throat muscles also constrict when fear sets in. If this happens to you, use the following exercise to relax the throat muscles.

    a.   Point your chin toward the ceiling, stretching the throat muscles as much as you can in this manner.

    b.   Place your tongue in the roof of your mouth and push with your tongue as hard as you can. Count: one thousand one, one thousand two, one thousand three, one thousand four, one thousand five.

    c.   Release the pressure being applied by your tongue and lower your chin, telling yourself to relax as you do so.

    d.   Repeat three to five times or until the tension in the throat muscles has dissipated.

For most people, using the RED technique will eliminate the light-headedness that results from the body's reaction to fearful thoughts. If it does not totally eliminate it, be prepared to use these coach-class relaxation exercises to increase your comfort.

Another Strategy for Controlling Your Breathing

The RED technique is recommended for controlling your breathing, but there is one additional breathing strategy you can use with ease. In the seat-back pocket in front of you on the airplane, there will be a small white bag that is placed there in case people get airsick. If your light-headedness continues, just place that bag over your nose and mouth, hold it tightly so no air comes in from the outside, and breathe normally. This will restore the oxygen–carbon dioxide balance in a matter of minutes. Why does this work? After you breathe into the bag for a few minutes, you are breathing almost pure carbon dioxide. The bag works, but most people are too embarrassed to use it. However, one participant put it this way, "If that is all I have to do to get rid of those dizzy feelings, I don't give a damn what the other people on the plane think." Most fearful fliers will not allow themselves the luxury of ignoring what others think.

SLOWING A RACING HEART

Another physical reaction to the automatic, scary thoughts about flying is a racing heart, which means that your heart rate may increase to two or three times its normal rate. The good news is that if you have good cardiovascular health, it could beat at this rate for days without injury to your heart. And there is more good news: the RED technique will slow a racing heart. However, all this good news may not be sufficient if you are a fearful flier whose fear is heightened thinking that your heart is literally going to burst because it is pounding so hard, or, as many people have described it: "It seemed that my heart was going to come out of my chest."

You can immediately slow your racing heart by using a technique that has been labeled the *Valsalva maneuver* after the physiologist who discovered it. Actually, Valsalva discovered a whole family of techniques to slow the racing heart, but only one of them will be described here because it can be used easily and unobtrusively on an airplane.

Caution: Consult with Your Physician

Two cautions are in order. First, the Valsalva maneuver is only for people who have healthy cardiovascular systems because the Valsalva maneuver can stop your heart altogether if you have a diseased cardiovascular system. The technique works by stimulating the *vagus nerve,* which regulates heart rate and runs the length of the body. However, if your cardiovascular system is diseased, the result may be stoppage of the heartbeat, so if you have any doubt about your health in this area, consult your physician. He or she may be able to recommend a similar technique that will work for you.

Second, while the Valsalva maneuver will lower your heart rate, it must be used with the RED breathing technique if you are going to maintain the gains you get as a result of using it. The epinephrine that caused the heart rate to increase in the first place is still in your system, and controlling your breathing will allow your body to eliminate it.

How It Works

Everything begins with the first frightening thoughts, which set the physical symptom in motion. When the thoughts come, your heart rate will increase instantaneously to 120–150 beats a minute. You decide that you want to lower your heart rate, so you take the following steps:

1. Sit erect in your coach-class seat. Take your pulse rate.

2. Force yourself to fill your lungs to capacity just as you did in the first step of the RED technique.

3. As you are filling your lungs, tuck in your tummy, that is, flatten it by pulling it in and up. Do not go as far as you did when you relaxed your diaphragm during the RED technique process.

4. When your lungs are totally filled, hold your breath, and using your stomach muscles, push down on your lower stomach (intestines) for five seconds much as you would if you were constipated. As you push, count: one thousand one, one thousand two, one thousand three, one thousand four, one thousand five.

5. Release the tension and exhale. Your heart rate will immediately come down about twenty beats per minute. Take your pulse.

6. Repeat the process. You will need to repeat it three to four times. Once you are comfortable with your heart rate, immediately use the RED technique to control your breathing. If you do not, your heart rate will accelerate again.

RELAXING TENSE MUSCLES

The process of relaxing tense muscles was described previously and will not be repeated here. However, you may have some muscle groups that become so tense that you need to apply the Identify-Tense-Relax (ITR) process. These muscle groups are the shoulder muscles and those at the base of the head and neck, which can be relaxed using the Turtle exercise; the temporomandibular joint (TMJ), the joint that links the lower jaw to the upper jaw, which can be relaxed using the Piranha exercise; and the upper legs and calves, which can be relaxed using the Ballerina exercise.

The trapezius muscles are the large muscles on the shoulders that support the neck. They, along with the muscles at the base of skull, are *stress susceptible*, as are the other muscle groups discussed in this section. Fortunately, this muscle group can be easily relaxed using the following exercise, which I call the Turtle:

1. Sit erect in your coach-class seat.

2. Simultaneously shrug your shoulders and pull in your neck like a turtle would if it was pulling its head into its shell. Try as hard as you can to pull your head in and touch your ears with the tops of your shoulders. Make your neck disappear.

3. Hold the tension and as you count—one thousand one, one thousand two, one thousand three, one thousand four, one thousand five—tilt your head backward and rotate it around to massage the base of the neck.

4. Release the tension at the count of five and tell yourself to *relax*. Just let your shoulder muscles fall back into a normal position and feel the muscle tension drain away.

5. Repeat three to five times or until the neck and shoulder muscles are soft and relaxed.

The Turtle is also a good exercise to use if you get tense driving an automobile. So is the Piranha. The TMJ can get so tense that it requires medication to relax in some instances. However, you can relax it by pretending you are a fish with an underbite—the Piranha:

1. Start by extending your lower jaw as far forward as you can, trying to extend it beyond the teeth in the upper jaw.

2. When you have extended it as far as you can, count: one thousand one, one thousand two, one thousand three, one thousand four, one thousand five.

3. Release the tension, tell yourself to *relax*, and let your jaw return to its normal position.

4. Repeat three to five times.

The muscles in the upper and lower legs frequently become very tense before and during a flight. I have seen this tension result in uncontrollable shaking of the legs. Even in this condition, your legs will support you if you need to walk around. However, you can take control of the tension by doing another coach-class exercise, the Ballerina. If you have ever watched dancers, particularly ballet dancers, warm up, you know they go through extensive stretching exercises to prepare their body for the rigors of dancing. In one of these exercises, they point their toes away from themselves and then rotate the foot to point their toes toward inward. This is exactly what you do in the Ballerina:

1. Slide your feet under the seat in front of you. There is not much room, so your feet will have to stay near the floor. Remember, this is a coach-class exercise.

2. Now lift one foot just off the floor, arch your foot, and point your toes away from you toward the front of the airplane (this will tense the large muscles on the top of the leg). Count: one thousand one, one thousand two, one thousand three, one thousand four, one thousand five.

3. Now rotate your foot so that your toe is pointing toward you (this will stretch the muscles along the back of the leg all the way to the buttocks). Try to point your toes at your chin and, as you do, count: one thousand one, one thousand two, one thousand three, one thousand four, one thousand five.

4. Now tell yourself to *relax*. Allow your foot to drop to the floor of the plane and repeat with the other leg.

5. Repeat three to five times with each leg.

The Ballerina will allow you to relax the tension in your legs to some degree. However, if the tension becomes painful and this technique is not working, go to the rear of the plane in the lavatory area and do some stretching exercises. The walk will be good for you because it will give you a sense of mastery of your environment. The exercises will help you relieve the tension, and doing them helps increase your feeling of control.

WHICH TECHNIQUES WILL YOU USE?

In the foregoing sections of this chapter, I have described a technique to stop your racing thoughts; one that can be used to control your breathing (actually two if you count the paper-bag method); a strategy that, when used with the RED technique, can be used to slow a racing heart; and the Identify-Tense-Relax technique that can be used to alleviate muscle tension. Which ones will you use? It depends entirely upon your symptoms. Table 2 lists symptoms that accompany the response to fear and how these symptoms can be controlled using the strategies that have been outlined in this chapter. Go through this table to identify how you react when you become fearful and the techniques you will need to help you master your fear on the airplane.

Table 2: Controlling Symptoms	
Thoughts	**Techniques**
Racing negative thoughts ("I'll die," "I'll suffocate," "I'll have a panic attack," "I'll be trapped," "I'll make a fool of myself.")	Thought stopping
Hypervigilant attention to details of the flight ("I am 'flying the plane.'")	Thought stopping
Superstitious thoughts ("I must call Mom in order to be safe.")	Thought stopping *and* RED (breathing)
Physical Symptoms	**Techniques**
Racing heart	RED

Tense muscles	Identify-Tense-Relax (ITR)
TMJ	Piranha
Shoulders/neck	Turtle
Legs	Ballerina
Chest	ITR
Stomach	ITR
Throat	ITR
Tapping feet	Ballerina
Awkwardness when moving about	Ballerina
Clenching of teeth	Piranha
Other Physical Symptoms	**Techniques**
Stomach upset	RED
Palms sweating	RED
Headache	Turtle *and* RED
Dizziness	RED
Mouth dryness	RED
Repeated trips to lavatory	RED
Stammering	RED

After you have identified your symptoms and the strategies that you are going to use on the plane to deal with them, begin to use these strategies in your everyday life to handle other stressors. Your thoughts about flying are automatic, and up to this point, you have been defenseless against them. Now you are arming yourself with ways to regain control of your thoughts and your body. Prepare for your next flight as though you were going to war.

AVOIDING AVOIDANCE

Avoiding avoidance is not so much a technique as a portion of the strategy that you need to follow as you battle your fear of flying. You "grow" your fear each time you avoid flying, and this, in turn, makes it progressively harder to fly. To fully consider what happens when you avoid a flight, imagine yourself in the following situation: Your boss calls on Wednesday evening and tells you that you have been selected to represent the company in San Antonio, Texas, on Friday. He has asked his secretary to arrange for the airline tickets and to make your hotel reservations. He also tells you that you can pick up the tickets in his office on Thursday. Your immediate reaction is to have fearful thoughts, and then the physical symptoms begin. On Thursday morning, your boss contacts you again and tells you that the meeting has been called off. What do you experience? You have an overwhelming feeling of relief! Your stomach is no longer tied in a knot. Your palms stop perspiring. The muscles in your back and shoulders relax, and you can concentrate on your work. Your body relaxes, and your mind stops focusing on flying.

What happens when you make a reservation, go to the airport, and then fail to board the plane? You get that same feeling of relief and perhaps the recurring thought that you just missed flying to your death. These feelings of relief are so powerful that they actually reinforce the negative thoughts and your avoidance of airplanes. Possibly worse, after you avoid, you will probably criticize yourself unmercifully, which lowers your self-esteem and weakens your ability to confront your fear in the future. The result is that the more often you give in to your fear, the more likely it is that you will avoid flying. After you have mastered the techniques outlined in this chapter, acquired the information in chapters 5–7, and prepared your own flight plan, it will be time to make a reservation and fly.

Do not plan to fly until you are reasonably sure that you will follow through with your plans. When you next make a reservation, you must be like the woman who put her arm through mine as we were approaching her graduation flight and said, "Duane, I'm going to the restroom and kiss my ass goodbye, but I'm getting on that plane." She admitted to a reporter who covered the seminar that she was totally frightened when she boarded the plane, but her admission was made with a relaxed smile on the return flight.

CHAPTER 5

Developing a Valid Information Base: Industry, Personnel, and Airplanes

You, like almost every fearful flier, have been told that flying is the safest mode of transportation available. The fact that you are still fearful means that you do not believe what you were told. There are two reasons why you are skeptical. One of these is the way the human mind works: after we develop a belief, we take in information selectively. In fact, we listen more intently to information that supports what we already believe than we do information that refutes our established beliefs. Second, all of us receive a great deal of misinformation from the media and from the people around us about airplanes, the personnel associated with the industry, and the industry itself, including some faulty information from people who should know better. There will be more about this later in this chapter and in subsequent chapters.

If you get on a plane and the flight attendants tell you, "We've been flying through thunderstorms all day," should you believe them? If a credible network journalist reports that a jet crashed because a mechanic installed bogus parts in the engines and that the problem is widespread, should you believe that the use of defective parts is a widespread problem? If you read in one of the most reputable newspapers in the country that there were hundreds of "near misses" in the skies across the country last year, should you believe the report? If you are truly a fearful flier, you will accept these reports as accurate.

All of these events were reported in these ways, and the reports were all misrepresentations of the truth:

- Flight attendants are taught nothing about flying or the policies that govern pilots. In fact, they likely know less about flying than you will after you read this book. Several fearful fliers told me that flight attendants have told them that they had been flying directly through thunderstorms. As you will learn in chapter 6, that could not have happened.

- On September 6, 1985, a Midwest Express DC-9 crashed after takeoff. It was widely reported that the crash was caused by the installation of faulty parts in an engine. Later the National Transportation Safety Board (NTSB) reported that, in fact, "a compressor spacer in the right engine had failed," and further investigation revealed that the assembly was not an FAA-approved part. Did this verify the report about faulty parts being the cause of the crash? Not quite: The NTSB reported that the crew made a mistake in dealing with the failed engine, and this contributed immeasurably to the crash. This very important fact was not included in the initial report because it came to light more than a year after the crash. Planes can fly quite nicely on one engine if the pilot makes the proper correction after an engine fails.

  Did the news agencies have an agenda? Perhaps they were trying to make the point that bogus parts were a problem throughout the industry. In fact, they were a problem for some airlines at the time of the report, but only for those airlines that subcontracted maintenance procedures to a few disreputable businesses. The problem was quickly identified and corrected. What should the news agencies have reported? "A Midwest Express DC-9 crash resulted because of the initial failure of an engine and an improper reaction by the pilot." That would have been objective reporting. (There are a number of citations online that pertain to this accident. For a synopsis go to http://en.wikipedia.org/wiki/Midwest_Express_Airlines_Flight_105.)

This story illustrates how the media distorts the news about air travel. My guess is that the distortions occur for several reasons, including premature speculation about the causes of crashes, failure to interview knowledgeable people, and the desire to increase television ratings or sales of newspapers. It is also the case that reporters hope to prompt the airline industry and agencies such as the FAA to increase airline safety. However, inaccurate reports unnecessarily frighten the unsuspecting public in the process.

- Some fearful fliers believe that midair collisions are commonplace. Is this belief accurate? Here are some facts. Commercial planes flying below 29,000 feet are spaced 1,000 feet apart vertically and 3–20 miles apart horizontally. Above 29,000 feet, planes are spaced 2,000 feet apart vertically and about 10 miles or more apart horizontally. Every plane flying over the United States is being tracked by an air traffic controller on a radar screen and simultaneously monitored via radar by a computer. When planes deviate from this spacing, the air traffic control (ATC) computer automatically registers it as a near miss. Are planes that are 800 feet apart in danger of colliding? Certainly not. Are planes that are 2 miles apart in danger of having a midair crash? Pilots laugh at this idea because they know the planes and passengers are in no danger. I am not suggesting that there has never been a near miss. Occasionally planes come within a few hundred feet of each other.

  According to FAA statistics (Federal Aviation Administration 2008), there have been a total of three midair crashes since 1982. And not one has occurred since 1991. Planes over the United States are on radar at all times and thus are monitored much as you are in your car when you pass through a highway patrol radar trap; a significant deviation from course results in an automatic fine for the pilot. These fines, which can reach $10,000, are paid by the pilot, not the airline.

The media thrives on airplane crashes and stories of near disasters because they generate readers and viewers. One journalist in one of my seminars told me that the people in his newsroom cheered when they learned that the crash of a DC-10 in Sioux City, Iowa, in 1989 had been captured on videotape. As you have undoubtedly noticed, stories of airplane disasters are reported over and over again. This produces another type of misperception: planes crash all the time. Newspapers and television stations even carry stories about the crashes on the anniversary of the flights. Several of the more dramatic accidents have been made into movies, one of which was about the aforementioned crash of the United DC-10 in Sioux City in 1989, which was one of the worst years for the airline industry in history. In that year, there were eleven crashes involving 278 fatalities (Federal Aviation Administration 2007). That is far too many, but that was five crashes out of nearly 7.6 million flights that originated in this country that year. I like the odds, particularly when you consider that on average, over the last decade, less than one hundred people have died per year in airplane crashes (with the exception of 2001, when a large number of people were killed in the terrorist attacks on the World Trade Center). In 2007, only one person died in an airplane crash while 30,401 people died in automobile crashes (FARS 2008). The information presented in this chapter and in chapter 6 was gathered over the past five years from the FAA (2007), *Fatality Analysis Reporting System Encyclopedia* (FARS 2008), and more than a dozen American Airlines pilots who have more than two hundred years of flying experience among them. In this chapter, I will answer questions fearful fliers most frequently ask about the airline industry, pilots and other personnel associated with the airline industry, and airplanes. Chapter 6 will address the questions most frequently asked about aerodynamics, flight planning, and the flight itself (including preparing for bad weather and turbulence). No attempt will be made to portray flying as perfectly safe. It isn't. It is simply one of the safest and fastest ways to get from point A to point B.

INDUSTRY

1. *How many flights originate in the United States and Canada each year?*
Few people are aware of the magnitude of the airline industry. Each year

more than 10 million flights take off and land in this country, and 1.5 million flights originate in Canada. One estimate by the FAA suggests that nearly one hundred thousand people are in the skies over the United States during the daylight hours each day.

2. *Is air travel really safe?* Arnold Barnett of the Massachusetts Institute of Technology and Mary Higgins of the Air Force Center for Studies and Analyses studied the safety records of the U.S. domestic airlines from 1977 to 1986 (Barnett and Higgins 1989). Their major conclusions were that the domestic carriers are the safest in the world and that they were four times safer in the decade studied than they were in the early 1970s. They also concluded that flying was ten times safer than it had been in the early 1960s. They estimated that the death-rate risk per flight was one in eleven million. Perhaps more importantly, air travel has become even safer since the Barnett/Higgins publication. The FAA at one time estimated that air travel is two hundred times safer than automobile travel, but a more reasonable estimate is that it is safer and more efficient because it is a highly controlled environment.

The probability that you will die in an automobile crash depends upon the nature of the automobile you drive (for example, SUV versus subcompact), your driving skill, when you travel, the highway conditions, and the drivers of the other cars on the road. Most fearful fliers create an illusion that they are "bulletproof" when they are driving their automobiles because they feel like they are in control. However, each day more than 80 people die on our highways. In 2006, 32 percent of these fatalities involved drunk drivers who ran into people who were in control of their cars but not in control of the drunk drivers (CDC 2007). The Centers for Disease Control and Prevention also reports that 18 percent of accidents involved people who were impaired because of drug abuse. Trains are very safe, and many fearful fliers choose trains over airplanes; some feel that they have some control if they are on board a train because they can stop the train and get off. However, in 2007, 4 passengers died and 990 were injured for every hundred million miles traveled (FARS 2007).

3. *Do all airlines have the same safety records?* There are at least half a dozen websites that rank the safety of air carriers in the United States and abroad. I have chosen not to list these because website addresses

change from time to time. However, by typing "safest airlines" into your search engine, you can find a list of safe airlines. I do want you to know that from 2002 to 2007, there were more than 65 million departures in the United States. The total flight time for these flights approached 125 million hours. There were ten crashes resulting in 109 deaths. In 2007, 30,401 people died in automobile crashes (Federal Aviation Administration 2007; FARS 2008).

I also want to point out that if you search some of the databases that rank the safety of airlines, you will find some that have downgraded American Airlines and United Airlines because they lost four planes in the attacks on the World Trade Center. Should United and American safety record rankings be lowered because of what happened on 9/11? Those crashes had nothing to do with pilot error, mechanical failures, or other factors associated with the airlines themselves. The failure for the 9/11 crashes should be placed at the feet of the FAA and local airport security in my view. The FAA was the federal agency charged with oversight of airline safety in general, and local airports were, for the most part, responsible for screening passengers prior to boarding. Screeners failed to locate the box cutters that were used as weapons by the terrorists, and the FAA failed in its responsibility to establish safeguards that would prevent takeovers by terrorists.

4. *Are commuter airlines as safe as the larger carriers?* I fly commuters. I feel much more secure on those commuter airlines offering jet service. My wife has chosen not to fly turboprops, a decision that I have not made. However, avoiding propeller-driven airplanes will not limit your lifestyle, and as regional jets replace turboprops, this will become a nonissue for most people.

5. *Is international flight as safe as flying domestically?* It depends on where your travels take you. If you travel on European and Pacific Rim air carriers, know that the safety records of these carriers are equal to those of carriers in the United States. However, the airlines with the worst safety records operate in developing countries in Africa and Asia. In 2006, the European Union banned 92 airlines from operating in EU airspace. Most of the banned carriers were of African origin, but some were located in North Korea, Afghanistan, Kazakhstan, Thailand, and elsewhere. A complete list of the banned airlines can be found on

BannedAirlines.org and BlacklistedAirlines.org. The current list bans all airlines from Angola, Equatorial Guinea, Indonesia, the Kyrgyz Republic, Liberia, Sierra Leone, Swaziland, the Democratic Republic of Congo, and Gabon (except for Gabon Airlines and Afrijet) (European Union 2008). The list also bans operations of eight individual carriers from Afghanistan, Cambodia, the Democratic People's Republic of Korea (North Korea), Rwanda, Sudan, and Ukraine. Because the list of banned airlines changes, you may wish to go to the European Union web page (www .euractiv.com/en/transport/airlines-banned-eu-skies-safety-concerns /article-177249) for current information.

6. *Are there ways to keep track of the safety records of various airlines?* Probably the best way is to subscribe to magazines such as *Traveler* and *Consumer Reports* because they periodically publish articles about airline safety. Some information is available from the NTSB website (www.ntsb. gov), but finding the information you seek may be difficult. However, keeping track of the safety records of individual airlines may not be necessary. If you fly on most U.S. carriers, Canadian carriers, European Union airline companies, and airlines located on the Pacific Rim (e.g., Japan, Australia), you are going to be on safe airlines. If you do have to fly on an airline that you are unsure of, call the NTSB and ask about the safety record of the airline in question, but do not expect an immediate answer. It also maintains information about the safety of foreign airports.

7. *What about charter airlines? Are they safe?* They are less safe than commuters (see PlaneCrashInfo.com at http://www.planecrashinfo.com /cause.htm) and than regularly scheduled air carriers, but they are still very safe. Charter carriers and air taxis fly under slightly different rules than do the regularly scheduled commercial carriers. Some of them have been cited for safety deficiencies. Here again, the best way to get information about a particular airline is to call the NTSB.

8. *Are there factors other than safety that should be considered when choosing an airline?* Research by airline companies suggests that the cost of the ticket is the primary basis for choosing an airline. However, because ticket prices and safety records are quite similar among the leading carriers, you may wish to consider factors such as service and the on-time record of the carrier. Airline companies seem to be competing for the airline with the

poorest service these days. Meals have been eliminated by most carriers except in the first-class cabin. Some airlines are beginning to charge for blankets and pillows, and most airlines are charging for checked baggage, particularly if more than one bag is checked. The service records of companies flying overseas are not readily available, but generally speaking, the people with whom I have spoken give European carriers higher marks for service than they give domestic carriers, and passengers rave about some of the Pacific Rim carriers such as Malaysia Air.

Statistics regarding on-time departures and arrivals and luggage lost are kept by the FAA and released on a regular basis (Bureau of Transportation Statistics 2008). Overall, about seven in ten flights arrive on time, with the smaller carriers reporting better on-time records than the larger airlines. However, for the first six months of 2008, US Airways had the best on-time performance with nearly 80 percent of its flights arriving on time. Conversely, the worst record was reported by American Airlines. Only a little over 50 percent of its flights arrived on time. NTSB also reported that about five passengers in one thousand filed complaints that some or all of their luggage did not arrive at their destination when they arrived.

9. *Are the airlines that file for Chapter 11 (protection against creditors) cutting corners on safety?* The idea that airlines that are in Chapter 11, which allows them to operate without having their creditors seize their assets, are unsafe probably developed decades ago with reports that Eastern Airlines' supervisors falsified repair records on some airplanes. It is probably worth reporting that when Eastern stopped flying, it was among the top-ten safest airlines in the world and that no accidents occurred as a result of the falsified repair reports. But the idea that someone would falsify repair records is troublesome.

To assess the risk associated with being in Chapter 11, it is important that you understand what occurs when an airline files for protection against its creditors. First, the FAA sends additional air safety inspectors to monitor that company. Second, the insurance companies of the airlines become involved in providing oversight of the day-to-day operation of that carrier. This occurs because they want to ensure the safest possible operation. At this time, most U.S. carriers have taken advantage of bankruptcy laws to keep themselves afloat during the years following 9/11. It is also the case that most have emerged from bankruptcy, and, while their balance sheets vary in financial health, they are operating successfully.

10. *What is the international language of the airline industry?* English is the international language. Pilots and air traffic controllers must be able to speak English. This facilitates communication when U.S. airlines fly to other countries and when foreign carriers come to the United States. If you are aboard an Iberian plane (the Spanish national airline) and it is flying to Spain, the crew and the air traffic controllers will speak in their native tongue, however. This will be true of any airliner traveling to its country of origin because this facilitates communication between the pilots and controllers.

11. *Is safety good business?* Many fearful fliers believe that the airline industry will cut corners and endanger their lives. This is flawed thinking. Consider that a crash may result in the loss of a plane worth from $20 million to $120 million. Further, if the airline company has been negligent, the liability suits can cost them additional millions. Safety pays huge dividends.

Factoid: According to information posted on the website PlaneCrashInfo .com, the probability of being involved in a crash resulting in a fatality is 1 in 6.06 million if you fly the twenty-five airlines with the best safety records. If you fly the bottom twenty-five airlines, the probability is 1 in 546,011. The probability of being killed in a single flight is 1 in 10.46 million in the twenty-five safest airlines and 1 in 723,819 in the twenty-five that are the least safe (PlaneCrashInfo.com 2006).

PILOTS AND PILOT TRAINING

1. *What is the background of the typical airline pilot?* Note that airline companies hire people who already know how to fly. The training that pilots receive after being hired focuses on how to fly commercial airplanes following FAA and company policies. Pilots come to the airlines from two sources: civilian and military training backgrounds. Most commercial airline pilots started their career in the military, but this is likely to change in the future because of the downsizing of the armed forces. Military pilots typically attend one of the service academies (e.g., Air Force Academy)

or complete ROTC training during their undergraduate education. After candidates for pilot training undergo a rigorous physical, they are selected for pilot training and, if they are able to complete that training, become military pilots. After completing their military obligation, most pilots have completed the necessary training needed to acquire an air transport pilot (ATP) license and have accumulated more than the minimum of 1,500 hours needed to apply for a position at a major airline.

The pilots who pursue the civilian route to becoming a commercial airline pilot may attend one of the colleges or universities that offer an undergraduate training program focusing on airlines technology (e.g., Florida Institute of Technology), or they may simply take advantage of the inexpensive flying lessons offered by many universities (e.g., Purdue University). These pilots will acquire a number of licenses on their way to the ATP license, including a single-engine license, a multiengine license, and an instrument rating that allows them to fly on *instrument flight rules* (IFR) as opposed to flying on *visual flight rules* (VFR). Civilian pilots may take a variety of jobs (such as being a flight instructor or flying cargo planes, corporate jets, or commuter airlines) on their way to qualifying to become a pilot for a major carrier. Ultimately, civilian and military pilots compete for the major airlines' jobs. While there has been some debate about which pilots are the best, the fact is that both routes produce good pilots.

2. *What are the characteristics of would-be pilots?* They are at least twenty-one years old, probably have a college education, and may have an advanced degree. They are mostly men, although more and more women are taking both the military and civilian routes to becoming pilots. They are typically in their late twenties and early thirties, in excellent health, have extremely stable personalities, and have accumulated more than three thousand hours of flight time. There are no inexperienced pilots in the cockpits of commercial airplanes in this country.

3. *What happens after they apply for jobs as airline pilots?* The companies begin the screening process by running extensive background checks on each candidate to verify their credentials. Then applicants are screened in several ways. They are given an extensive battery of psychological tests to assess aptitude and the stability of their personalities. They are also placed in a simulator and asked to demonstrate that they can fly. A

preliminary review of the candidate's family health history is also made. If there is a family history of heart disease or other debilitating illness, it is unlikely that the candidate will be hired. Finally, they are subjected to a rigorous interview by a panel of pilots.

4. *What is the nature of the initial training pilots receive?* New-hire pilots enter older, established companies such as United, American, or Delta as first officers. The captain is in charge of the crew, the airplane, and the cargo. The first officer, who alternates flying the plane with the captain, sits in the right seat in the cockpit (the captain is in the left seat).

The training that pilots receive is increasingly computer assisted, that is, teaching programs have been developed that contain the information pilots need. The computer "teaches" the lesson to the pilot and administers a computerized test to assess whether the pilot has learned the material that was presented. However, once the computer has completed its work, the pilot must undergo a rigorous oral examination administered by the FAA representative or company instructor who has been appointed by the FAA (called a *check airman* even if she is a woman) to verify that the knowledge has been acquired.

The final phase of the training is *simulator training.* Simulators are exact replicas of the airplane cockpit that the new-hire pilot will operate. They are called simulators because they can simulate all aspects of flight, including takeoffs, landings, and emergencies such as engine fires. In the simulators, new hires must demonstrate that they can perform their jobs to the satisfaction of the FAA or an FAA-appointed simulator instructor (also called a *check airman*).

Unlike many other industries, the airline industry trains new-hire pilots to proficiency, which means that the new pilot must demonstrate that he or she can handle every aspect of the job to the satisfaction of the instructors. After simulator training is completed, new-hire pilots are assigned to the plane for which they were trained. For the first fifteen to twenty-five hours in their new positions, they are supervised by a company check airman to make sure that they can perform satisfactorily.

New-hire pilots are placed on probationary status for one year at most airlines. At the end of each month, they are evaluated by the captain of the crew with which they have been flying. If these evaluations are satisfactory and new-hire pilots maintain their proficiency, probationary status is removed.

5. *Do pilots have to return for training after they are hired?* No group of professionals has more continuing education than pilots. Some airlines require captains to return for *recurrent training* every twelve months. During this recurrent training, pilots go to their company's training center for extensive retraining regarding all aspects of their job. First officers also return to their training centers for recurrent training once per year. During these training periods, the captains and first officers must demonstrate that they are proficient in all aspects of flying the plane. During recurrent training, all crew members are updated on any new developments in the industry, but more important, they are checked to see how they function in the case of abnormal or emergency situations. Because emergency situations are so rare in airplanes, recurrent training is the only way that pilots can maintain their ability to deal with them.

If pilots or first officers fail to demonstrate that they can perform either routine or emergency procedures, their training will be continued until they reach proficiency. If they cannot perform satisfactorily, they are dismissed from the airline. The bottom line is that all the people who fly commercial airplanes must put their job on the line at least once a year. Do any of them fail recurrent training? Not many do because they are so carefully selected at the start, but a few do, and they are dismissed.

6. *How does a first officer get to be a captain?* The answer to this question is quite simple: seniority. Airline captains must retire at age sixty although a retirement age of sixty-five is being considered. Retirement creates opportunities for first officers to advance to captain. As you might imagine, one of the reasons crew members want to advance is pay; captains make more money than first officers.

Once a crew member qualifies by virtue of seniority to advance, he or she must go back for what is termed *upgrade training*. This lasts for varying lengths of time depending on whether the person is upgrading to a different airplane or is simply switching to another position on the same plane.

7. *Are pilots qualified to fly more than one plane?* Generally speaking, they are not. Because the cockpits of airplanes vary, a decision was made to restrict pilots to flying one type of plane to enhance safety. However, there are at least two exceptions to this rule. The cockpits of the Boeing

757 and 767 are identical. Pilots who qualify to fly one of these planes are qualified to fly both. Similarly, the cockpits of the family of B-737s are identical, and thus pilots who are qualified to fly the 737-200 are also qualified to fly 737-400s and 737-800s.

8. *How is work in the cockpit coordinated?* I have already mentioned that the captain is in charge of all aspects of the flight. This does not mean that he or she can ignore the input of others. Several years ago, a plane landed in the wrong city. Although no one was hurt, there was a thorough investigation revealing that the first officer knew they were landing in the wrong place but had been ordered to keep his mouth shut by a dictatorial captain. This and other incidents convinced the FAA and the airlines that they needed to alter the way the cockpit crews functioned. All domestic airlines have adopted a training program called Crew Resource Management. In training, captains are taught how to involve their crews in the decision-making process.

9. *What about pilots' health? I worry that they will get sick during the flight.* The rules regarding physical checkups are the same as they are for recurrent training: captains must have complete physicals twice per year and first officers must once per year. After the age of forty, pilots' physicals must include an electrocardiogram (EKG). To eliminate the possibility that a friendly family physician might not report the results of the physicals accurately, these examinations are administered by an FAA-appointed doctor. The results of the EKGs are transmitted directly via telephone to Oklahoma City, Oklahoma, where they are interpreted by an FAA physician. The airlines go so far as to specify that when the pilots are eating during a flight, they each be served a different meal in the off chance that one of the meals would result in illness.

10. *Does the use of drugs and alcohol by pilots endanger the flying public?* Drugs and alcohol are two separate issues with the same implication: pilots who use them are impaired and cannot operate a plane safely.

Pilots caught using illegal drugs are dismissed immediately. As noted earlier, one part of the screening process for new hires is a drug test. If pilots fail the test, they are not hired. After hiring, pilots are subject to random drug testing and testing "for cause." For example, pilots involved in accidents are tested routinely.

Random drug testing typically works as follows: (a) a computer randomly selects employees to be tested, (b) an official from the airline meets the incoming plane and informs the pilots that they are to be tested and specifies when and where the testing is to occur, (c) the pilot shows up at the appointed place and provides a urine sample (if the pilot has just gone to the lavatory, the testers wait until a specimen can be provided), (d) the specimen is divided into two samples so that a second test can be run if the first is positive, and (e) the samples are sent to a laboratory for testing. If the sample is positive, the pilot can appeal. For example, a pilot who had eaten poppy seed rolls during his flight tested positive, early in the drug-testing program. Eating poppy seeds or drinking certain herbal teas produces what are termed *false positives*. Another pilot who had been injected with a morphine-based anesthetic in his visit to the dentist also tested positive. Both were cleared of drug usage. However, if pilots test positive for drug use, their flying careers are terminated.

How many pilots have tested positive? American Airlines, which has nearly eight thousand pilots, has never had a positive test. Other airlines report similar results. Most pilots say that illegal drugs are not a problem in the cockpit. Based on everything I have learned, I concur with that assessment.

You may also be interested to know that there are severe restrictions on the legal drugs pilots can take and still fly. Pilots may take legal drugs containing barbiturates, codeine, and other similar substances if prescribed by a physician, but they cannot fly while they are taking the medication. There are even restrictions on the over-the-counter drugs that a pilot may take while operating an airplane.

But what about alcohol abuse? Weren't three Northwest Airlines pilots caught drinking illegally? Yes, they were. Three members of a Northwest crew were drinking in a Moorhead, Minnesota, bar the night before they took a flight from Fargo, North Dakota, to Minneapolis, Minnesota, where they were arrested on March 8, 1990. This highly publicized case led to additional scrutiny in this area and ultimately to the adoption of a random alcohol-testing program that began in January 1995. However, in 2002, two Air West pilots were arrested and charged with drinking within six hours of attempting to fly their plane from Miami to Phoenix. Their licenses were immediately revoked. They were subsequently tried and convicted in 2005. The pilot was sentenced to five years in prison. The first officer received a prison sentence of two years and six months.

The FAA rule is that pilots may not drink eight hours before a flight, and many companies have stricter policies. For example, some airlines prohibit pilots from drinking twenty-four hours before a flight and while they are on *layovers* (rest stops that are required for pilots who are assigned to what are termed *multiple-day trips*). After several hours of flying, the FAA requires that pilots be permitted to rest. This typically occurs in a city other than the one in which the pilot is based. Pilots flying internationally fly from their bases to foreign destinations such as London or Tokyo and then lay over to rest before flying back to their bases in this country.

I examined the NTSB accident reports dealing with the period of 1982 to the present. Please note that there is no single report summarizing accidents involving drugs and alcohol, so it was a matter of sifting through a variety of documents. My finding: no commercial airline accident occurred because of pilots' consumption of alcohol or illegal drugs. But what about those Northwest pilots? They were drinking a few hours before their flight and thus violated the FAA eight-hour rule as well as their company's rule of not drinking twelve hours before a flight. They were reported by a patron in the bar where they were drinking, met by federal officials at the conclusion of their flight, arrested, and subsequently tried, found guilty of breaking a federal law, fined, and sent to prison. Moreover, their licenses to fly were suspended and their careers terminated. Because captains flying for major airlines make from $75,000 to $200,000 per year, the drinks these pilots had were among the most expensive in history. Most pilots won't go into a bar dressed in their uniforms and fastidiously avoid breaking the rules.

Until January 1995, airlines depended on self-monitoring and crew monitoring to control alcohol abuse in the industry, and these are still important safeguards against drinking on the job. By "self-monitoring" I mean that pilots are expected to monitor their own behavior and seek help if they begin to abuse alcohol to the point that it influences their functioning in the cockpit. Crews are also charged with monitoring each other. If a captain or first officer knowingly flies with a person who is drinking, he or she can, and in all probability will, be dismissed from the job along with the offending crew member. A flight attendant who knows that one of the pilots has been violating the rules is also obligated to report that person. Additionally, the FAA and some companies operate what some pilots refer to as 1-800-SNITCH lines that can be used by crew or members of the public to report pilots who violate either the drug- or alcohol-use regulations.

11. *Are pilots supervised on the job?* As already stated, the captain is in charge of the crew and has oversight responsibilities. However, captains and crew are given no-notice line checks, both by the FAA and company supervisors. The way this works is that the person who is going to perform the line check simply shows up, presents his or her credentials, and states, "I will be flying with you today." During this line check, the functioning of each crew member is monitored, along with the teamwork of the crew. Feedback about their functioning is provided at the end of the flight. In the unlikely event that some unusually bad practice is observed, the supervisor has the prerogative of sending one or more crew members back to their company's training center for additional training. Importantly, every captain must have at least one line check each year or the captain's license is suspended until the check can be scheduled.

12. *What about stress? Are many pilots overworked and is flying a plane a high-stress occupation?* Research has shown that certain parts of flying are quite stressful, particularly those segments of the flight involving takeoffs and landings. To reduce this load, the captain and the first officer alternate flying various segments, or *legs,* of the flight. However, the stress experienced by pilots is not due to danger. It is related to the workload during takeoffs and landings. When you are considering the stress an airline pilot must endure, it may be useful to consider that the FAA restricts pilots to flying one hundred hours per month, and union contracts often restrict the number of hours flown to as little as seventy-five hours per month. The amount of flying time is measured in minutes from pushback from the jet bridge to return to the jet bridge—so only the time when they are actually operating the aircraft is included, not the time spent waiting for passengers to board. The result is that sometimes pilots put in very long days, and while the FAA requires that they be given adequate time to rest before they fly again, the job can be quite tiring. It is also the case that pilots who make transcontinental and transoceanic flights are dealing with the stressors associated with adjusting to different time zones.

Although the jobs of pilots of major airlines are stressful, generally speaking, this is probably compensated for by relatively short work weeks. On the other hand, pilots for many of the commuter airlines fly the maximum amount of time allowed by law and make many take-offs and landings during the time they are flying. There is an ongoing concern that stress and fatigue may represent a major problem among these pilots. The FAA is currently considering revising the rules that govern commuter-pilot working conditions.

13. *What about the pilots on those long transoceanic flights? Don't they get tired? I've even heard stories that they sometimes go to sleep.* The airline industry is aware that fatigue can be a major problem on long flights. For this reason they put an extra pilot on flights to Europe and an extra crew member on longer flights to places like Tokyo. Additionally, seats in the passenger cabin are reserved for the crew on some planes so they can rest. In the Boeing-built B-747-400, bunks are provided.

In spite of these efforts, there have been documented cases of crew members going to sleep on these long flights. The FAA is now considering letting crew members take catnaps during these long flights to keep them refreshed. Of course, one crew member would remain awake to fly the plane.

Should you worry about the crew sleeping? You should not worry for a second. There has never been an accident involving a U.S. carrier that was due to the crew sleeping. The fact is that the plane is on autopilot for most of these long flights anyway, and the crew's chief responsibility is to monitor the autopilot.

PERSONNEL OTHER THAN PILOTS

1. *How are mechanics trained and supervised?* The training and selection of mechanics is very much the same as for pilots. Mechanics come to the airlines after being trained in the military or attending an FAA-approved civilian school. They often start with smaller airlines and work their way up to major airlines. They are drug tested just as pilots are, and their work is subjected to the same level of scrutiny. For example, after a repair is completed on an airplane, the mechanic who made the repair signs the plane's log book and places his or her employee number

beside the signature. Then a supervisor checks that the repair has been made properly and also signs the log book and places his or her employee number beside the signature. If that repair fails, the mechanic and the supervisor are subject to fines as large as $5,000, and there is no guesswork about who is responsible. To keep up to date and to maintain their skills, mechanics undergo rigorous recurrent training on an annual basis. You should also be aware that the FAA provides oversight for mechanics and the repair process.

2. *What is the function of flight attendants?* Most people are surprised to learn that the primary job of flight attendants is to ensure the safety of the passengers. If you have flown, you know that they read a set of safety instructions regarding seat belts, flotation devices, and the use of oxygen masks before each flight. You also know that they check to make certain that passengers have their seat belts fastened before each flight and that the tray that is in the back of each seat is in the upright position. You may not be aware that the announcement "Flight attendants, prepare for departure" is a signal for the flight attendants to arm the emergency slides so that in the event of an emergency, the slides will deploy and passengers can be evacuated safely. It is even less likely that you know that flight attendants are trained in first aid procedures, but that they are precluded from using the equipment and medication that is on board every flight. However, in the event of a medical emergency, one of the flight attendants will ask if there are medical personnel on board who can assist with the emergency. If this fails, the flight attendant will inform the captain that a medical emergency exists and the captain will land the plane at the first available site where the passenger can get assistance.

Finally, by now you have probably guessed that flight attendants' training focuses more on safety than it does on providing service. For example, flight attendants must demonstrate that they can evacuate a plane in ninety seconds with half the exits blocked. They also return once per year for recurrent training that focuses on safety. People who have been in emergency evacuations report that the flight attendants work well under the pressure of evacuating a plane.

3. *How are flight attendants supervised?* FAA and company representatives observe flight attendants without their knowledge. Individuals or crews that function improperly can be fined or dismissed.

4. Are the air traffic controllers competent? When Ronald Reagan was president, he fired the striking air traffic controllers. Supervisors and replacements from the military were brought in to substitute for the controllers who had been fired. This led to a persistent and reoccurring rumor that air traffic controllers are incompetent and thus there is increased danger of midair collisions. I discussed the possibility of midair collisions earlier in this chapter and will not revisit it here except to say that your chance of being struck by space junk returning to earth is probably greater than your chance of being in a midair collision. However, know that current air traffic controllers are well trained and supervised and that many of the problems (e.g., on-the-job stress) that brought about the strike during the Reagan era have been resolved. One accident has been attributed to the ATC since Ronald Reagan left office.

Some thought is being given to hiring recent high school graduates, and that has been a source of worry for some people. My concern is about maturity and training, not age.

One of the major safety advances that has occurred is that the number of airplanes that can be safely handled by the ATC at a particular destination has been established. Once the airways approaching an airport are "saturated," that is, are filled with all the planes that can be handled safely by the ATC, no additional planes are allowed to enter that airspace. For the most part, this means that delays are now experienced on the ground instead of in holding patterns around the airport. This is safer, and it is also more economical because of the fuel used in holding patterns. But what happens if a thunderstorm develops and the airport at your destination is closed after your plane is en route? The captain may be asked to slow the speed of the aircraft, fly *vectors* (a zigzag path), or wait in a holding pattern for a short period of time. All of these maneuvers are perfectly safe. And yes, planes have enough fuel to fly vectors or to hold, a topic to be addressed in greater detail later in this chapter. Here is the most important point: air traffic controllers do not accept more planes into their airspace than they can safely handle.

5. I have heard that air traffic controllers do not have the most up-to-date equipment available to them. Is this true? It was true twenty years ago, but it is no longer accurate. The FAA was slow to require that equipment such as computers and radar systems be updated. The result was that there were more delays than would have been the case if the best equipment had been at their disposal.

AIRPLANES

1. *I know that some of the airplanes being flown by the airlines are thirty years old. Aren't they dangerous?* This is the number one question about airplanes asked by fearful fliers, and the answer is a resounding "No!" Most fearful fliers think of airplanes as they do their cars. Automobiles wear out after so many years and miles. So do airplanes, but there is one significant difference: The airlines engage in preventive maintenance on an ongoing basis and completely overhaul airplanes on a regular schedule, based on flight time or every four to five years. The modern jetliner receives eleven hours of maintenance work for each hour it is flying. Commuter planes, which are smaller, receive six hours of maintenance work for each hour they fly.

As I stated in chapter 1, I visited the American Airlines facility in Tulsa, Oklahoma, to view the renovation of the airplanes firsthand. This facility can handle as many as thirty-six jetliners at one time. In the first building we visited, a DC-10, which can carry more than two hundred people, was being redone. The landing gear had been removed, as had all the engines, many of the control devices on the wings, and the interior of the plane.

The process is to inspect each part and bring it in line with new specifications. For example, engine parts that are subjected to great heat and begin to deteriorate are heat-treated to restore the molecular structure of the metal in the parts. They are then rebuilt piece by piece and painstakingly tested. At the end of this process, a flight crew tests the plane and checks to determine that it is operating properly. Then the plane is placed back in service essentially as a new plane. The price tag for this process is $1 million or more.

During my visit, I also learned that oil samples are taken regularly from the engines of each plane and analyzed to determine if they contain telltale ingredients that indicate the engine is about to fail. More impressively, the functioning of the engines of some planes is monitored by computer as they fly, and the data is analyzed to determine if the engine is functioning normally. If there are any signs that an engine is not functioning properly, it is removed prior to failure.

Tire wear and pressure are checked routinely before each flight as are all systems and instruments on the airplane. For the captain to fly a plane, all parts on the *minimum equipment list*, such as the autopilots, altimeters, fuel gauges, and landing gear sensors, must be in working order. If you experience a delay because of a mechanical problem, it is because a part or system is not functioning properly.

2. I have heard that planes have a lot of backup systems so that if one fails, another is available. Is this true? "Redundancy" is the watchword when airplanes are built. They are equipped with spare altimeters, compasses, autopilots, weather radar, hydraulic pumps that operate the control devices, at least two systems that can be used to lower the landing gear, and so on. Also, planes have at least twice the power that they need to fly, and thus, if an engine fails at the most critical time in the flight, the plane can fly quite nicely on one engine on a two-engine plane, two engines on a three-engine plane, and three engines on a four-engine plane.

3. Are the manufacturers of airplanes regulated? They are, absolutely! The FAA provides standards that must be met in the building of airplanes as well as inspectors who ensure that the standards are met. However, airplane manufacturers routinely exceed FAA standards in the manufacturing process. For example, the FAA requires that airplanes used in commercial air travel remain airworthy even if a hole develops in the plane, which has happened from time to time in the history of commercial aviation. In the past, planes that had rather large holes in them continued to fly and landed successfully. Additionally, the FAA requires that the wings of an airplane support at least one-and-a-half times the weight of the plane, but aircraft manufacturers exceed that recommendation. A fully loaded B-747-400 may weigh nearly 1,000,000 pounds on takeoff if it is fully loaded with fuel. The wings on that plane will support in excess of 2,000,000 pounds. Other planes are built to similar specifications.

4. Are some planes safer than others? There is widespread belief, even among pilots, that some planes are safer than others, but this belief is not rooted in objective data. I have searched. All airplanes that carry passengers must meet certain minimum FAA specifications.

5. *Do planes have specialized safety equipment?* Yes, they do. Here is a partial list:

- *Ground proximity warning system:* This system has been installed on all jetliners that fly in this country. Its function is to warn the pilot if the plane is coming dangerously close to the ground. It does this via a female voice that says, "Pull up, pull up."

- *Wind-shear detection devices:* This system warns the pilot if the plane is in a dangerous weather condition called wind shear. Again, a voice comes on and says, "Wind shear, wind shear." This is the signal for the pilot to take evasive action.

- *Traffic alert and collision avoidance system (TCAS):* This system has been installed on all jetliners. Its purpose is to back up the ATC system and avoid midair collisions. It monitors other airplanes in the vicinity of the plane, and if a collision is imminent, gives the pilot directions on how to avoid it.

- *Weather radar:* The crew has access to weather information from several sources including their own radar. They are taught to interpret radar so that they can avoid thunderstorms and other dangerous weather conditions.

CHAPTER 6

Developing a Valid Information Base: Aerodynamics, Flight Planning, Weather, and Miscellaneous Concerns

This chapter picks up where chapter 5 left off, providing you with a valid information base about flying. In this chapter, the topics of aerodynamics (what makes planes fly), flight planning, and weather will be discussed, as will some miscellaneous issues that fearful fliers often ask about.

AERODYNAMICS

1. *How can anything as large as an airplane stay in the air? It seems unnatural.* Planes have four forces at work on them as they fly: (1) *drag*, due to wind resistance; (2) *thrust*, which comes from jet engines or propellers; (3) *gravity*, or the pull of the Earth; and (4) *lift*, which comes from the action of the wings. An airplane will fly if it has large enough wings that can be pushed through the air fast enough by its engines so that it can overcome the forces of drag and gravity. As one pilot of thirty years put it, "Give me big enough wings and engines, and I will fly the Empire

State Building to London." However, for our discussion, you need a little more information than this.

Thrust from a jet engine is produced because the engine *ingests* air through the front of the engine, compresses it, heats it (which causes it to expand), and then expels it through the rear of the airplane. This is not unlike what happens when you blow up a balloon and then release that balloon into the air.

Propellers, which are driven by jet engines on many commuter planes, also produce thrust. The wing produces the lift needed to literally raise the plane off the ground by developing what is termed a *pressure wave*. A pressure wave, which is a condensed column of air, is created when a wing is pushed through the air at high speed at a certain angle of attack. This is something like flying a kite: the pressure of the wind keeps the kite aloft much as the pressure wave created by the plane allows it to remain airborne. The pressure wave travels with the plane as it passes through the air and always stands between the plane and ground. As the plane moves faster, the pressure wave intensifies, and the plane is lifted higher and higher. Speed increases the size of the pressure wave as does the size of the wing being pushed through the air. When the plane reaches the desired altitude, the pilot makes adjustments in the speed, the angle of attack of the wing, or both, and the plane levels off. When pilots wish to descend, they can slow the speed by pulling the throttles back to idle and reducing the pressure wave. One pilot we worked with always told the fearful fliers in our classes to imagine their planes riding on solid columns of air. It may help you to imagine this same thing because that is virtually what happens.

The people who manufacture airplanes take advantage of the principle of the pressure wave to develop wings so that very large airplanes can fly at relatively low speeds. Remember, lift results from a wing being pushed through the air, and the resulting pressure wave is determined by speed, the size of the wing, and the angle at which the wing passes through the air. Manufacturers influence the intensity of the pressure wave by placing devices on the wings that can increase the size of the wing as well as the angle of attack. These devices are called *flaps* if they are located on the trailing edge of the wing. Some airplanes have moveable devices, known as *slats*, on the front of wings. If you have flown, you have probably observed these parts on the wing move as the pilot prepares for takeoff and again during the landing approach. The takeoff speed for many planes is about 150 miles per hour. The flaps, slats, or both increase the curvature of the wing so that the plane will be able to "lift off" at this speed. As soon as the plane gets into the air, it accelerates, and the curvature of the wing is reduced. This is done by retracting the flaps and slats on the wings. Ultimately, these devices are retracted altogether because the wing can produce enough lift to keep the plane in the air without them, given that lift increases geometrically with speed. This means that a wing will produce four times as much lift at 200 miles per hour as it will at 100 miles per hour. Once the slats and flaps are retracted, the wing produces plenty of lift to keep the plane in the air.

2. *What if an engine fails just as we lift off? Will we still have enough thrust to push the plane through the air?* In chapter 5, I covered the issue of how planes are built and I said that one of the FAA requirements for commercial airplanes is that two-engine planes must be able to fly on one engine if the other engine fails at the most critical portion of the flight. This provision includes takeoffs. Therefore, if an engine fails just as the pilot begins the liftoff, the plane will still fly safely. In recent history, both Delta and US Airways planes have literally had engines drop off during takeoff with no adverse consequences.

What happens if an engine fails? The pilot will return to the airport and land as quickly as possible to maximize your safety. You are in no danger during this return to the airport.

3. *What if both engines fail on takeoff?* Quite simply, the plane is going to come down. The odds against both engines failing on takeoff are in the trillions, however. In recent history (the last thirty years) there are two incidents in which both engines failed on takeoff. A Scandinavian Airlines plane crashed because large quantities of ice were ingested on takeoff due to improper de-icing. Under current de-icing regulations, that could not occur in this country. I'll address this topic more fully later in this chapter. On January 15, 2009, US Airways Flight 1549 departing from New York City's LaGuardia Airport encountered a flock of large birds, some of which were ingested into both engines of the A320, causing them to fail. The pilot landed the plane in the Hudson River.

4. *What if both engines fail when the plane has reached its cruising altitude?* Many fearful fliers, particularly those who are afraid of heights, worry about the plane falling out of the sky because of engine failure,

developing a valid information base   73

turbulence, or wings coming off. These things do not happen, but let me answer the question with a question. How many engines does the space shuttle use when it returns to Earth? The answer is, "None." It glides back to Earth and lands with no engines. Commercial airliners are much better gliders than the space shuttle. They have a glide ratio of about 15 to 1, which means that for every foot they are in the air, they can glide 15 feet. Remember the Scandinavian Airlines plane that crashed because the engines ingested ice? As noted radio announcer Paul Harvey says, "Now I'm going to tell you the rest of the story." All of the people on that plane survived the crash. The engine failures occurred at about 3,500 feet. The pilot was able to maneuver the plane to miss some houses and landed the plane in an open field. The newspapers called this crash a Christmas miracle. The second miracle occurred when all 155 of the passengers and crew survived the US Airways crash on January 15, 2009. Like most modern-day "miracles," these planes' landings were due to the skills of the pilots, the fact that airplanes do glide, and, yes, a great deal of luck.

A plane flying at 35,000 feet can glide 525,000 feet (99.43 miles) if both engines fail. In many parts of the United States, there would be a landing strip available to the pilot within 99 miles. If you fly up and down the East Coast, get a window seat and make an X on a napkin every time you pass over an airport or the pilot makes an announcement that you have just passed over a city that has an airport. In some parts of the United States, the plane could be landed on a superhighway. This is illegal, but I have been told by more than one pilot that given the choice between being fired and a crash, they will take the former. *Translation:* The modern airline pilot wants to survive as much as you do and will land on a superhighway if no other alternatives are available and that option presents itself.

5. *What if we are flying over water and the plane has to land because of engine failure? Will the plane float?* Fearful fliers leave no stone unturned when thinking about the problems that can befall them when they are on airplanes. "Ditching" is the term used to describe landing an airplane on a lake, river, or ocean. As noted earlier, a domestic commercial jet-liner, US Airways Flight 1549, ditched on January 15, 2009. Commercial air carriers from other countries (e.g., Japan) have made water landings. Modern jetliners will float if they land on water so long as they remain

intact. The A320 that was ditched on January 15, 2009, stayed afloat long enough for all passengers and crew to be evacuated safely.

6. *I've heard the word "stall." Doesn't that mean that the plane is going too slow and is about to fall out of the sky?* When the wings of the plane are not moving fast enough through the air to produce the lift needed to keep the plane airborne, *stall* occurs. It should be comforting to know that pilots are as concerned about stall as you are and that devices in the cockpit monitor the speed of the aircraft to make sure that stalls do not occur. As a result, they are very conservative in computing the airspeed needed to keep the plane flying at all times other than touchdown. For example, prior to each takeoff, pilots compute the speed needed to lift the plane safely off the runway. This computation is based on the weight of the aircraft, cargo, and passengers as well as weather conditions. In this computation, and all others regarding flying speed, pilots use a safety margin of 30 percent. If the plane will lift off at 120 miles per hour, they set the takeoff speed at 156 miles per hour. You should also know that there is a stall-warning device in the cockpit that alerts the crew to the possibility of a stall.

7. *What is the most dangerous part of the flight?* Pilots have a quick answer to this question, "The trip to the airport." Most fearful fliers have another answer, "The takeoff," but they are incorrect. They are certain that this is the most dangerous part of the flight. Conversely, they love landings because they will be back on terra firma and safe from the dangers of flying. Research by Boeing Corporation suggests that 30 percent of accidents occur on the takeoff and cruise to altitude and 61 percent occur during the descent and landing. The remainder occur during the cruise phase of the flight.

FLIGHT PLANNING AND THE FLIGHT ITSELF

1. *Who plans the flights? It all seems to be so chaotic.* The flight planning is conducted initially by a person called a *dispatcher*. The dispatcher's job is to check weather reports as well as reports of turbulence and to select a route for the flight. The dispatcher also checks the *load* (projected weight

of the plane) and determines the fuel required for the flight. Ultimately, the dispatcher develops a *flight plan* that contains weather information, an estimate of the turbulence en route, the weight of the aircraft (including the fuel), and anything unusual about the departure and landing airports, such as closed runways. The flight plan also includes information about alternate airports, if any. Each flight must have an alternate airport if (a) there is the possibility of bad weather that might delay landing or close the airport altogether or (b) the airport to which the flight is going has only one runway. In some instances, a flight will be assigned a second alternate if there is a chance the first alternate would be unavailable because of weather. Once the dispatcher develops a flight plan, it is fed into the FAA computers so ATC can approve it. This allows ATC to regulate the flow of traffic taking off and landing at all airports, as well as the traffic on the various air routes.

Approximately thirty minutes before the flight, the flight captain prints out the flight plan and reviews it. If the information is not to his or her liking, changes (e.g., in amount of fuel) can be requested. Ultimately, the dispatcher, captain, and ATC must agree on the information in the flight plan before the flight can be declared legal. Once the captain agrees with the flight plan, he or she signs it to signify acceptance. As you will see later, the flight plan is flexible and can be changed if bad weather develops en route.

2. *Are there rules that govern flight plan development?* Absolutely, and a list of these rules follows:

- A flight cannot be dispatched into areas of heavy turbulence.

- A flight cannot be dispatched into a thunderstorm.

- To be legal, a domestic flight must have enough fuel on board to fly to its destination and land. However, in determining the fuel load, many factors are considered. First, the weight of the airplane is calculated because the heavier the plane, the more fuel required. Second, the weather en route and at the destination is considered. Since planes are not allowed to fly through thunderstorms, if one or more storms are expected during the flight, additional fuel is placed on board so the pilot will be able to fly around them. If bad weather is possible at the destination, one or more alternate airports must be chosen in case the plane cannot land at its destination. In this situation, the plane must have enough fuel on board to go to the primary destination, travel to the most distant alternate destination, hold for forty-five minutes, make a missed approach, and then make an approach and land. Planes flying international routes have enough fuel on board to fly to their destination, make a missed approach to land, fly to their most distant alternate destination, hold for thirty minutes, and land with 10 percent of their en route fuel still in their tanks.

- A plane cannot be legally dispatched unless all equipment on the minimum equipment list is functioning.

- When flying easterly headings, planes at cruising altitudes fly at odd-numbered altitudes (35,000, 37,000, 39,000, and so on). When flying in a westerly direction, planes must fly at even altitudes (24,000, 26,000, and so on).

3. *I worry about the plane running out of fuel, particularly when we have delays. Is this a realistic worry?* There have been instances when planes ran out of fuel, but most of these cases involved third-world airlines or highly unusual situations. Please consult the preceding question and then think about this question. Fuel planning is done very conservatively, as you can see.

4. *What happens if bad weather develops en route?* The captain is in charge of the flight and of any changes that occur after the plane takes off. If bad weather is detected on the radar, the pilot contacts ATC and requests an alternate route, which is provided. The pilot may also contact the dispatcher for advice on this matter.

5. *I don't like to fly to Europe or Asia because we spend so much time over water. What can I do?* You do spend a lot of time over water on such a flight, but only one U.S. commercial air carrier has landed in water. All passengers survived. It may also be helpful for you to know that you are never very far from land, particularly when you fly to Europe. When you look at a map of the world, it is usually flat and it looks like

a pilot would fly straight across the Atlantic Ocean to London or other European destinations. But find a globe and try to locate the shortest route to London. You will see that it parallels the coast of Canada, is near Greenland, and, in fact, is never far from land. Now here's a little bit of trivia. If you fly to Hawaii, the halfway point between Los Angeles and Honolulu is the point at which you are farthest from land no matter where you fly in the world.

6. *Why do they allow planes with two engines to fly to places like Hawaii and Europe? Wouldn't it be safer to fly a plane with four engines, like the B-747?* No, it wouldn't be safer. Engines are so reliable that many pilots will never experience an engine failure in their careers. That is why planes with two engines have been approved by the FAA for flights to Europe.

7. *Are there any differences in safety between flying at night and flying during the day?* No, night flying is just as safe as flying during the day. Some fearful fliers like to fly during the day so they can keep an eye on the ground. Others like to fly at night so they cannot tell how far up they are. You will realize that your fear of flying is behind you when you don't worry about when you fly or what equipment you are on and you do not watch the weather forecast.

8. *Why do planes fly so high?* Many fearful fliers would feel better if the plane flew closer to the ground. The fact is that this would make the flight less safe for a number of reasons. First, there are fewer planes at higher altitudes and so the risk of midair collision is eliminated when planes fly at higher altitudes. Second, the higher a plane is flying, the farther it can glide in the one-in-a-trillion chance that all engines should fail. There is one other reason why jets fly at high altitudes: jet engines run more economically at higher altitudes than they do at low altitudes.

9. *You keep saying that every aspect of the flight is monitored. What do you mean by that?* I do keep insinuating that the flight of a commercial airliner is one of the most carefully monitored operations that you can imagine. Let's consider a typical flight. After all passengers are on board and in their seats, a flight attendant must inform the pilot that everyone is seated. It is illegal for the pilot to move the plane with anyone standing. Before the plane can be moved from the jet bridge, permission must be gained

from ramp control. Once the plane is pushed back from the jet bridge, the pilot must obtain permission from ground control before he or she can begin to taxi. Once the end of the taxiway is reached, the pilot must get clearance from the airport control tower to taxi onto the runway and take off. After takeoff, the pilot must receive permission from ATC to deviate from the flight plan that was filed prior to takeoff unless there is an emergency. During all phases of the flight, including the taxi out in major airports, the plane is on radar. Its speed, course, and altitude are recorded every step of the way. Additionally, instruments on the plane monitor every aspect of the flight and record them. The cockpit voice recorder records every word that is said in the cockpit. If pilots make errors, such as flying too fast or wandering off course, they do not have a conference with a member of the highway patrol—they are automatically subject to discipline. This is the equivalent of you being monitored automatically from the moment you get into your car in your garage until you arrive at work, day after day after day. In some areas, automobiles are monitored in somewhat the same manner as airplanes. For example, in many municipalities, cameras photograph the license plates of automobiles that run red lights, and computers mail citations to the automobile owners.

10. *I've heard that pilots are risk takers. How do I know that they are attending to the business of flying the plane?* After the crash of an Eastern Airlines airplane in a swamp outside of Miami, the NTSB investigation revealed that the crew had all become involved in trying to locate the source of a problem that had developed and that no one was really attending to flying the airplane. Subsequently, the FAA mandated what is called a *sterile cockpit period*, which begins with departure from the jet bridge and continues to 10,000 feet and begins again at 10,000 feet on descent and ends when the plane is safely parked at the jet bridge. During this period, the crew cannot be interrupted by the flight attendants, are prohibited from making announcements other than those that pertain to the safety of the flight, and must refrain from engaging in conversations other than those related to the flight. Remember, everything said in the cockpit is recorded, and, in the case of an accident, the cockpit recorder is used to determine what occurred in the cockpit. Also remember that pilots are professionals. They will obey the rules not only because their job and their own safety are involved, but because they have pride in doing a job well.

WEATHER

1. *Do many airports have trouble with fog limiting the visibility of pilots? Is it safe to land in low visibility?* The general rule here is that if the pilot is making the landing, it is safe to do so. However, the rules governing low-visibility landings are complex. First, these rules depend upon the nature of the runway. If it is equipped with an electronic *glide slope* (the path the plane takes as it prepares to land), a low-visibility, instrument landing is possible. Second, pilots with little experience are restricted to making landings when the *ceiling* (the distance between the base of the clouds and the ground) is at least 300 feet. Third, the equipment on board the plane is a factor. Some planes are equipped to land in *0/0 conditions*. This means that they can land with zero ceiling and zero forward visibility as measured by an instrument on the runway. Ultimately, 0/0 will mean just that: no ceiling and no forward visibility.

2. *How is a 0/0 landing possible?* Electronic glide slopes and autopilots make this possible. The autopilot interprets an electronic signal from the glide slope and keeps the plane on course while it controls the speed of the airplane using autothrottles. The autopilot also adjusts the control surfaces on the wings as the plane lands and applies the brakes on landing. The pilot's job is to monitor the operation (and yes, there is more than one autopilot).

3. *What about ice on the planes?* I know some accidents have been caused by failure to de-ice planes properly. Air Florida (1982, Washington, DC) and Continental Airlines (1987, Denver, Colorado) have had crashes that were linked in part to faulty de-icing.

Current rules governing de-icing should completely eliminate icing as a problem. As of 1993, the composition of the fluid used to de-ice planes changed: the ratio of glycol de-icing fluid to warm water increased. Further, after planes are de-iced, they are coated with a solution that keeps ice from forming for a longer period of time than was previously the case. Additionally, the amount of time between de-icing and takeoff has been reduced. Finally, visual inspections of the areas of the planes that are susceptible to icing have been increased in the period prior to takeoff. The FAA and the airline industry can be criticized for not implementing these steps prior to 1993, but the important point is that they have been implemented.

4. *What about ice on the runway? Isn't it hazardous to land when the runways are slick?* Unsafe runways are closed until they can be cleared by removing the snow or by other means. Also, as snow and ice develop, crews inspect the runways regularly to determine whether they are safe. Finally, planes are equipped with antilock/antiskid braking systems that prevent the brakes from locking up and causing the plane to skid.

5. *What about ice that develops on the wings of airplanes after takeoff?* Icing during the flight can be a problem for some small planes, but not for the modern jetliner. Why is this? Airplanes that fly using jet engines (as opposed to those using jet engines to turn propellers) circulate heat from those engines through the wings and other areas that might collect ice. Smaller, propeller-driven planes do not have this system. However, almost all planes have very effective in-flight de-icing systems.

6. *What about thunderstorms? Aren't they dangerous?* Yes, thunderstorms are dangerous. The center of a thunderstorm contains high winds, hail, and heavy rain. The industry's approach to dealing with them is avoidance. At altitude, commercial aircraft must remain 20 miles from the core of a thunderstorm. The *core* is defined as the red area that you see on your television screen when watching a weather report and that pilots see on their weather radar.

Many people report flying through thunderstorms. They tell of seeing lightning, hearing thunder, and being in heavy rain. They are probably right; it is legal and safe to fly in what appears on your television screen as the light green, dark green, and yellow areas of a rainstorm. However, pilots will not fly in the red area because it is illegal, and they avoid as much of the yellow areas as possible because they want to give you a comfortable ride.

7. *What would happen if you inadvertently flew into a thunderstorm?* That isn't going to happen, but I asked some pilots this question. They respond that the plane would take the stresses of the storm, but the passengers would be very uncomfortable. If you really want to know how a plane would function in a thunderstorm, obtain a copy of the videotapes that have been made by the hurricane hunters. Once every six hours, the U.S. Weather Bureau sends a reconnaissance plane into each hurricane to take readings of wind velocity, barometric pressure, and other indicators of the intensity of the storm. These planes must fly through embedded

thunderstorms and high winds. The crew looks like they are in a blender, but the plane survives quite nicely. You also need to know that the planes used by hurricane hunters are not specially built for the purpose of flying into thunderstorms.

8. *What happens if lightning strikes a plane?* The fact is that lightning will probably strike a plane somewhere in the world today and every day. The plane will survive with no ill effects because it is not grounded (has no connection to the earth). The people on the plane will be scared because the lightning strike is likely to be accompanied by a flash and a loud peal of thunder. If this happens to you, just tell your neighbor (and yourself), "It's okay; planes get struck every day. They aren't grounded."

9. *I've heard that wind shear is associated with thunderstorms and that it can cause accidents. Is this true?* Technically *wind shear* is a condition in which the wind direction, the velocity, or both change rather dramatically in a short distance and time span. Wind shear at higher altitudes is not dangerous. However, wind shear at lower altitudes presents a potential hazard to airplanes, and it is often associated with thunderstorms. Actually, there is a special and very dangerous type of wind shear called a *microburst* that is most worrisome. The type of microburst most often described in the media begins with a strong headwind and is followed by a tailwind, torrents of rain, and a strong downdraft that literally slams the plane into the ground if the pilot does not take evasive action, but there are many other types of microbursts that can be equally dangerous. A microburst caused the crash of a Delta Airlines L-1011 in Dallas, Texas (1985), and more recently, the crash of a US Airways DC-9 in Charlotte, North Carolina (1994).

The airlines and the FAA have instituted several measures to help pilots deal with wind shear. One change is in the training pilots receive. Currently, pilots are taught to recognize wind-shear conditions in flight simulators and to avoid them by taking evasive action. Once each year, pilots take refresher training in making these maneuvers. Additionally, two wind-shear detection devices have been developed. One of these is a device that measures wind direction. This device is placed around a runway; when it detects the presence of wind-shear conditions, air traffic controllers are warned. The second detection method is to use Doppler radar. It seems likely that the crash of the US Airways plane in

Charlotte, North Carolina, would have been averted if the airport had been equipped with Doppler radar, which is now the case. Information about the seriousness of the wind shear in the area was not relayed properly to the pilots, and the pilots flying the plane made a serious error when they reacted to the wind shear. US Airways has revamped its training procedures to help its pilots deal more effectively with wind shear.

Should you worry about wind shear? I do not believe that you should for two reasons. First, there is probability: in the last decade there have been more than 125 million airplane takeoffs and landings in this country, and not one plane has been lost to wind shear. Second, many pilots believe that the likelihood of a wind-shear accident happening in the future is practically nil. US Airways was criticized by the FAA because of the training it provided to its pilots, and the company has improved in this area. Procedures for informing the pilots about the presence of wind shear have been improved as well. Doppler radar is available at all airports, and the development of new detection devices for onboard use should eliminate wind shear as a safety hazard.

10. *I worry that pilots are pressured by their companies to fly in bad weather to maintain schedule. Is this true?* No, it is not. Once the captain signs the flight plan, he or she accepts full responsibility for that flight. In operating the flight, the captain has the following concerns, in order of priority: safety, passenger comfort, and schedule. Captains are required to make responsible decisions, but because of their training and professionalism, decisions regarding safety are rarely questioned unless they make a mistake that results in an accident. Most importantly, they are not hassled by their companies about on-time arrivals.

TURBULENCE

1. *What causes turbulence?* There are a variety of factors that cause turbulence, but please understand first that turbulence is air in motion. Perhaps because they cannot see it, people imagine that air currents blend smoothly, but this is not the case. To help you visualize turbulence, imagine putting a hose into a swimming pool, turning it on, and watching the water: the water moves just like two streams of air coming together. These are the causes of turbulence:

- In our country, the prevailing wind direction is from west to east. As the wind encounters mountains, trees, and even buildings, it is forced to rise, and in doing so, displaces other air, causing it to move.

- Thunderstorms have tremendous amounts of energy and generate changes in air currents, which in turn causes other air to move.

- When a cold front from the north encounters warm air, the cold air (which is heavier) displaces the warm air, causing it to rise. This produces rain and also puts air into motion.

- On a warm day, the sun warms the soil, causing moisture to evaporate, and air to rise (convective heating). As this air rises, it causes other air to move.

- The jet stream, at least on the edges where the jet stream is moving faster than the air around it, causes other air to move.

- When an airplane passes through the air, small whirlwind-like vortices spiral off the wing tips, displacing other air and thus setting it into motion.

2. *Does turbulence pose a threat to airplanes?* No, it doesn't! Most fearful fliers believe that during turbulence, the wings may come off or the pilot will be unable to control the plane and it will go spiraling into the ground. To those of you who believe this, I challenge you to identify one U.S. plane that has been knocked out of the sky by turbulence. Earlier I indicated that the companies that manufacture airplanes exceed safety recommendations regarding the strength of their parts and that airplanes fly into hurricanes without being damaged. If planes can survive those stresses, they will not be harmed by the relatively minor turbulence they encounter in the course of routine flights.

3. *But I have read stories about people being injured by turbulence. What happened?* It is not always possible to predict turbulence. Typically, turbulence occurs over mountain ranges, near thunderstorms, and over very warm areas, such as Phoenix in the summertime. However, there is a

phenomenon known as *clear air turbulence* (CAT), which, while it is often associated with sharp turns in the jet stream, can occur in other situations. A plane can fly into CAT, and passengers who are not belted into their seats can hit the ceiling or have hot coffee spilled on them. That is why you are advised by the pilot to keep your seat belt fastened. That is also why experienced fliers hang onto a seat back as they walk around the cabin. You need not fear turbulence, but you should be prepared for it. It is always possible that turbulence will be encountered.

The next time you read about passengers being injured in turbulence, look carefully to see if some of the injured were flight attendants. They are in the greatest jeopardy when a plane hits turbulent air because they are not seated. Do not be alarmed if the pilot asks the flight attendants to take their seats. This is being done for their safety, not because some terrible catastrophe is about to befall the aircraft.

4. *Is it possible to measure turbulence?* Pilots are provided with a turbulence index for each segment of the flight on every flight plan. The index used for these estimates ranges from 1 to 6. You will never experience level 6 turbulence because it is illegal to dispatch a plane into it. However, I will provide you with your own turbulence meter so you can measure the turbulence you experience. On your next flight, ask the flight attendant to bring you a glass of water. Place it on the tray in front of you. If there is nothing more than an occasional ripple on the surface, you are flying in level 0 turbulence. If the ripples become more frequent but the water does not spill, you are in level 1 or 2 turbulence. If the water begins to slosh out of the glass, you are probably in level 4 turbulence. In level 4 turbulence you will feel the plane move from side to side a bit, and you may seem to move upward against your seat belt. I repeat, you are in no danger, but I cannot guarantee that you will be comfortable.

5. *How do pilots feel about turbulence?* Typically, pilots don't like turbulence, not because it is dangerous but because they are professionals who want to give you a comfortable ride. They will do their best to find an altitude that is relatively smooth, and you may feel the plane climb or descend as they change altitudes to find smoother air. The one exception to this rule came from one pilot who flew planes to Tokyo at the end of his career. He confessed that he actually enjoyed a little "light chop" because it restored circulation to his backside after he had been sitting for a while.

6. *I have read about planes that were upended because they landed too close to others. Why did this occur?* Wing-tip vortices, which spin off the tips of the wings of large planes, can be forceful enough to upend small planes. This is a problem on landing. However, wing-tip vortices move or dissipate fairly quickly, so planes are spaced from two to five minutes apart to eliminate the threat caused by wing-tip vortices. If you are landing behind a small plane such as a Boeing 737, you will be flying approximately 3 miles behind it. If you are flying behind a Boeing 757, 767, or 777, Airbus A380, or other "heavy" airplane, the spacing will be greater, probably at least 5 miles.

7. *What is an air pocket?* An air pocket is a figment of a journalist's active mind. The term "air pocket" was apparently coined during World War I by a reporter trying to describe turbulence. Many fearful fliers believe that there are "holes in the sky," which, if flown into, will cause the plane to fall hundreds if not thousands of feet. There are no air pockets.

8. *If there are no air pockets, why do planes fall hundreds of feet?* It is literally impossible for a plane to fall hundreds of feet even though it may seem to you and to others that you are falling long distances. The only reliable indicator of how far a plane moves in turbulence is the altimeter located in the cockpit. I have talked with pilots (with, collectively, hundreds of years of flying experience) about planes falling. Most of them have never seen the altimeter move more than 20 feet in the heaviest turbulence. One reported a movement of 50 feet. That is really not very far when a plane is flying at 35,000 feet.

It is also important to note that planes do not fall in turbulence in the sense that an elevator might fall, that is, they do not go straight down. A plane is moving forward at a speed of 450–550 miles per hour when flying at altitude. What happens to a plane in turbulence is not unlike what happens to you when you pass over a speed bump in your car. The car keeps going forward. One difference between the operation of your car and the operation of an airplane is that a speed bump or a pothole can cause the car to careen off the road. Planes have no such problem.

9. *Do pilots have trouble keeping planes under control in turbulence?* The image that many people have of the cockpit comes from movies that depict the pilot struggling with the yoke to maintain control of the plane

in turbulence. In fact, the plane is on autopilot when flying through turbulence because autopilot can sense the changes that are occurring in the air currents and make changes to compensate for them. However, pilots are perfectly capable of flying the airplane in all situations, including turbulence, and keeping it under control.

MISCELLANEOUS CONCERNS

1. *I have heard that the quality of the air I breathe in an airplane is so poor that I might get ill. Is this true?* In the last decade, many concerns have been raised regarding the quality of the air people breathe in an airplane. Here are some facts:

- You should know that the air in an airplane is fresh air, not bottled air. It is brought into the airplane through the engines and dispersed through the air conditioning system. Old air is let out of the plane through a valve in the rear of the plane.

- The air is changed in the plane every three to ten minutes, depending upon the type of airplane.

- The pilots breathe the same air as the passengers.

- The Centers for Disease Control and Prevention in Atlanta, Georgia, has determined that you are at no greater risk of contracting a communicable disease on an aircraft than you are in other places you visit. To be sure, you can catch a cold from the person next to you on an airplane, but you can also catch a cold if you visit an elementary school classroom.

There is one major problem with the air in planes: low humidity. Drink lots of water, lighten up on the alcohol, and, if you wear contacts, take them out because they will dry out and make you very uncomfortable. All these steps will help you adjust to the low humidity. It is also the case that the carbon dioxide level in planes exceeds that found in fresh air. The result of breathing this air for long periods of time can be headaches and fatigue, particularly on long flights.

2. *How can we still breathe when we are flying at 35,000 feet?* It is true that you could not get enough air into your lungs to survive at 35,000 feet unless some steps were taken to help you. To make sure that you can breathe, the cabin is pressurized by restricting the outward airflow. This allows you to breathe normally. Actually sitting in an airplane at 35,000 feet is about the same as visiting the foothills west of Denver, Colorado; the "altitude" of the cabin is about 6,500 feet.

3. *What if the pressurization system fails?* Failure of the pressurization equipment is rare, but it does happen. In this event, an oxygen mask drops out of an overhead compartment or the seat back in front of you. Place this over your nose and mouth and breathe normally. Immediately after depressurization, the pilot will take the plane down to an altitude that will allow you to breathe normally, typically at 10,000 feet or less. I once flew from Atlanta to Raleigh–Durham on a plane that had broken pressurization equipment. We flew at an altitude of 7,000 feet and were perfectly comfortable.

4. *I have heard that airplanes sometimes fly into flocks of birds. Is this true, and if so, what is the result?* It is true that planes fly into birds from time to time. The result is typically a dead bird and the odor of burned feathers in the cabin. However, according to preliminary reports, a flock of large birds resulted in a double bird strike and the crash of US Airways Flight 1549. Airplane engines have been improved to the point that they can ingest large birds and continue to function. In fact, engines are tested by firing dead chickens into them. However, they are not foolproof.

What is being done about the problem? The FAA requires that aircraft engines be able to sustain a strike with an 8-pound bird and still remain airworthy. Manufacturers exceed this requirement! Airports use a variety of approaches to scare birds away, including firing cannons and employing dogs to chase birds that nest or roost near the runways. Also, the weather radar on airplanes will detect flocks of birds in time to allow pilots to take evasive action. Even the safety of birds is considered.

There have been other bird strikes in the last forty years, but the US Airways crash on January 15, 2009, was the first time a plane has been downed by birds since I began tracking airline accidents three decades ago.

5. *Where is the safest place to sit on an airplane?* When fearful fliers ask this question, they usually mean, "Where is the safest place to be in a crash?" First, all places on an airplane are safe, but the FAA told me that no one place is safer than another in a crash. Over 50 percent of people involved in crashes survive no matter where they are sitting (PlaneCrashInfo.com 2006).

6. *Are some airports safer than others?* There are consistent rumors that some airports are unsafe. This is simply untrue. The FAA would close an unsafe airport. *Do some airports require a pilot to exercise more skills than others?* Pilots think that New York's LaGuardia Airport and DC's Ronald Reagan Washington National Airport fit into this category. *Does this make them more dangerous?* One pilot who was asked this question responded by saying, "I've landed airplanes on aircraft carriers. Now that requires some skill." The point is this: some airports require more skill during landing and takeoff, but they do not come close to exceeding the skills of the pilots who take off from and land at them every day. The stories about dangerous airports were written by uninformed journalists who often use faulty databases for their articles.

7. *What if there is an emergency when the plane is in the air?* There are two types of emergencies that might occur—one involving a passenger and one involving the plane. As you know, the pilot will land the plane at the nearest airport if a passenger becomes ill. The same is true if a mechanical problem develops. The pilot may or may not inform you of the emergency, depending on the workload in the cockpit. I'm sure you would rather have the crew attending to business in the cockpit than talking to you!

8. *How likely is it that I will be in an emergency evacuation?* In the first edition of this book, I estimated that about thirty emergency evacuations occurred per year. That estimate was based on the 1987–1993 period. Hynes and Associates (1999) collected data from the FAA, insurance companies, and the airlines when they examined the number of emergency evacuations from 1988 to 1996. They concluded that, on average, fifty-eight planes per year underwent an emergency evacuation and that about 4,800 people per year were involved. On average there were about eight million flights per year during this period (Federal Aviation Administration 2008).

9. *How can I avoid an injury if I am in an emergency evacuation?* Earlier I recommended that you pay very careful attention to the flight attendants in these situations because they are well trained to handle evacuations. Some other recommendations include:

- Take off your high heels and panty hose. High heels may catch on the slide or injure others. The panty hose will melt on the slide and give you a bad burn. Also remove rubber-soled shoes. They have a tendency to catch on the slides and cause people to tumble. Keep your shoes so that you can put them on quickly once you have been evacuated.

- Wear clothing to cover all bare areas, especially below the waist. Never board a plane wearing shorts or a miniskirt. Do not put your hands down on the slide as you evacuate. Instead, fold them across your chest or hold them above your head. This will prevent you from getting painful abrasions from rubbing your hands against the slide.

- Wear cotton clothing. It will not melt and is less likely to tear on the slides.

- Once you are out of the plane, move quickly away from it. Many injuries occur because evacuating passengers run into people in the evacuation area.

- Forget about your belongings. Worry only about getting yourself out of the plane.

- Put infants in a car seat. It costs more money, but if the plane stops suddenly, it is unlikely that you will be able to hold onto a child in your lap or arms.

- If there is smoke in the plane (which is very, very rare), don't drop to the floor as you have been taught to do in a household fire. Instead, bend over and lower your head to the point that it is about as high as your waist. This will allow you to be mobile and to avoid the most noxious smoke.

10. *Why do they make the announcement to turn off nonapproved electronic devices just before takeoff and during descent?* Some electronic devices such as CD players, cellular phones, and personal computers interfere with the navigational devices used by pilots. This interference, while potentially dangerous, has never caused an accident, but it has caused missed approaches and "go arounds." This interference is only a problem at low altitudes when very precise navigation is required and thus these devices can be used safely at altitudes above 10,000 feet.

CHAPTER 7

Developing a Valid
Information Base: Terrorism

The history of Islamic extremists' attacks against airliners began on July 23, 1968, when a group representing the Popular Front for the Liberation of Palestine (PFLP) successfully hijacked an El Al B-707. The El Al flight, which was bound for Rome, was diverted to Algeria where forty days of negotiations began. Eventually twenty-one passengers and crew who were held hostage were set free, as were the hijackers. El Al was targeted again later that year (December 6, 1968) when the PFLP attacked an El Al plane in Athens, Greece. A mechanic was killed. There was another attack on El Al in Athens in 1969. In December 1969 in Zurich, Switzerland, an El Al copilot was killed and a pilot was injured by terrorists. There were other 1969 attacks on El Al offices and facilities, but the attacks aimed at airplanes ended on September 6, 1970, when two terrorists failed in their attempt to hijack an El Al B-707. These and other incidents involving El Al are chronicled on Wikipedia (2008). In 2008, El Al was selected as the world's safest airline according to an article in the *Jerusalem Post* (*Jerusalem Post* staff 2008). I'll explain why it went from being one of the world's most beleaguered airlines to one of the safest later in this chapter.

TERRORIST ATTACKS

Terrorist attacks on airplanes are not a new safety issue in this country. In fact, the incidence of terrorist attacks has decreased sharply, as is illustrated in the following list. I have included terrorist attacks in this list that were discussed in the first chapter. I have also included some relatively recent incidents involving attacks or planned attacks that occurred in Great Britain and might have implications for Americans. The nature of the incidents and the airlines involved are included in this list, as are the cities from which the flights originated or where the incidents occurred:

2007—London/Glasgow: Eight people, at least two of whom were physicians, were arrested. They were allegedly involved in bungled car bombings focused on terminals in Glasgow and London. An SUV was rammed into the air terminal in Glasgow. When the bomb in the SUV didn't detonate, two terrorists set fire to the vehicle.

2007—Havana: Plane hijacked (no takeoff; hijackers captured).

2006—United Kingdom: Twenty-one people were arrested. They planned to blow up as many as ten planes flying principally from the United Kingdom to the United States.

2003—Havana: Two planes hijacked on separate occasions (Aerotaxi).

2002—Havana: Plane hijacked (private plane).

2001—Paris (de Gaulle): Shoe bombing attempted (American Airlines 63).

2001—Boston, Massachusetts: Attacks on World Trade Center North and South Towers in New York City (American Airlines 11 and United Airlines 175).

2001—Washington, DC (Dulles): Attack on Pentagon (American Airlines 77).

2001—Newark, New Jersey: Attempted attack thwarted by passengers near Shanksville, Pennsylvania (United Airlines 93).

2001—Florida, rural airstrip: Plane stolen (private plane).

2001—Marathon, Florida: Plane stolen and probably taken to Havana (private plane).

2000—Cuba: Plane stolen (Cubana).

1996—Cuba: Plane stolen (Aerotaxi).

1996—Madrid: Plane hijacked (Iberia).

1996—Cuba: Plane hijacked (Cubana).

1993—Cuba: Plane hijacked. Landed in Miami (private plane).

1992—Cuba: Plane hijacked (private plane).

1988—Lockerbie, Scotland: Bomb explodes in midair (Pan Am 103).

1987—San Luis Obispo, California: Disgruntled employee killed pilots and manager (Pacific Southwest).

1987—Cuba: Plane hijacked (Cubana de Aviacion Antonov).

1986—Karachi: Attempted hijacking (Pan Am).

1985—Athens: Terrorists shot at plane and threw grenades (TWA).

1980—New Orleans, Louisiana: Plane forced to fly to Havana (private plane).

1973—Rome: Terrorists threw incendiary grenades (Pan Am).

1972—San Francisco, California: Plane hijacked (Southwest).

1970s—Various locations: Thirty-two flights hijacked that landed in Cuba or the United States.

1960s—Various locations: Fifty-one flights hijacked that landed in Cuba or the United States.

1950s—Miami, Florida: Two flights hijacked, one bound for Havana, one for Miami.

Please note that nearly one hundred acts of terrorism involved Cuba and, most often, Cuban citizens who wanted to come to the United States or go to Cuba for a host of reasons. In most instances, when the hijackings involved passengers on commercial airliners, the planes landed safely and the passengers were released unhurt. The hijackings in the middle of the twentieth century and the resulting safe landings and passenger releases led to an airline philosophy that suggested that when a plane is hijacked, the best strategy is to appease the hijackers. On September 11, 2001, that philosophy was abandoned and a new era in dealing with terrorism began.

Preventing Terrorism

Clearly the most appealing approach to preventing terrorism begins before passengers board their flights. The United States and Western European nations use sophisticated surveillance methods that target potential terrorist activities. This is our first line of defense. I included the two incidents in the United Kingdom in the list to illustrate how law enforcement officials in the United Kingdom were able to apprehend potential terrorists before hundreds, perhaps thousands, of people were killed. In this country, the Federal Bureau of Investigation (FBI) and the Central Intelligence Agency (CIA) have their efforts focused on preventing attacks on commercial air carriers. However, it is clear that the CIA and FBI missed many clues that an attack was in the offing prior to 9/11.

Vigilance in the civilian population is another key to stopping terrorist attacks. An excellent example of how civilians can play a major role in detecting terrorist activities is illustrated in the foiled plot to kill soldiers at Fort Dix, New Jersey. Brian Morgenstern, a Circuit City employee, processed a videotape that had been brought to his store to be converted to a DVD. The tape contained images of men at the Pennsylvania State Game Land in Gouldsboro firing what appeared to be semiautomatic weapons and shouting in Arabic, "God is the greatest." He called the local authorities who involved the FBI. An FBI informant penetrated the group and was instrumental in helping the FBI get videotape of the group's planning activities. Consequently, six terrorists were arrested in the case before the group could take action.

If you have visited an airport recently you are aware that there are periodic announcements asking that you report any suspicious activities to the authorities. It is a request that all fliers should heed.

El Al's Security System

For a passenger's view of the El Al screening process, consult V. Walt's article in *USA Today* (Walt 2001). El Al's strategy for protecting its ground personnel, planes, crews, and passengers begins in the general boarding area. Uniformed and plainclothes security guards, both armed, patrol the terminal looking for explosives or any behavior that looks suspicious. Passengers are asked to report to the terminal three hours before their flight departs for check-in and interrogation. Each passenger is interviewed individually and asked their point of origin, reason for their trip, occupation, and whether they packed their own luggage. El Al officials do not believe that most potential terrorists can remain calm under intense questioning. Each interviewer is trained to evaluate what officials of the airline term "microexpressions." These are brief facial expressions that last less than a quarter of a second and often appear involuntarily. An interviewer trained in detecting microexpressions can often identify emotional responses.

Once the interview is completed, the passenger's ticket is stamped and he or she is free to check in. A passport monitor checks passport information against the files of international law enforcement agencies. Luggage is screened in three ways: x-rayed, hand searched, and tested in a decompression chamber. The decompression chamber is used to check for bombs that might be detonated by the decompression of the aircraft. Luggage searches are conducted by El Al security agents in Israel and other countries. It is the only airline that uses decompression chambers to check for bombs and sends its own agents to airports throughout the world to personally search luggage.

El Al's security system extends to its planes. Air marshals carrying firearms are assigned to every international flight. Each airplane's cockpit is equipped with double doors. Only personnel with a secret code may enter the first door. The second door is opened only after the first door is closed and the captain or first officer has identified the person seeking entrance to the cockpit. After an attempt was made to shoot down one of its airliners using a handheld antiaircraft missile, El Al equipped its planes with an infrared antiaircraft missile device named Flight Guard. The system uses Doppler radar to detect incoming missiles, either from the ground or from hostile aircraft, and deploys flares as decoys. The

Flight Guard system is a first for El Al, and it remains the only carrier at the time of this writing to utilize the system (Reuters 2006).

The major criticism of the El Al security system has been that it employs racial profiling with the result being that Muslim passengers are sometimes singled out for more intense questioning and inspections. El Al company officials have defended their system, but the Israeli Supreme Court ruled in April 2008 that the practice was illegal. El Al has altered its screening procedures somewhat, but critics charge that the changes are superficial (Barham 2008).

The U.S. System

As has already been noted, the U.S. system begins with surveillance by the CIA, FBI, local law enforcement officials, and the general public. After 9/11, the responsibility for airport security was turned over to the Transportation Security Administration (TSA), with the exception of a few airports left in the hands of private companies who now work for the TSA. The TSA is charged with developing and implementing policies and procedures to protect travelers in all modes of public transportation. Five types of TSA personnel work to protect the traveling public:

1. *Transportation security officers* control entry and exit points in the airport including the parking area just outside the terminal.

2. *Federal air marshals,* working in plain clothes, blend with passengers to identify and defeat potential terrorists. Air marshals are assigned to some flights based on intelligence information and risk assessment.

3. *Transportation security inspectors* conduct inspections of passengers, luggage, and cargo.

4. *Behavior detection officers* (BDO) have a role similar to that of the El Al officials who watch for suspicious behavior. As was the case in Orlando, Florida, on April 1, 2008, people who are acting suspicious are flagged for additional screening. In Orlando, the BDO identified a suspicious-looking passenger and alerted the baggage screeners. Luggage X-ray screeners found the components of a pipe bomb in the subject's suitcase.

Please note that the material in the man's luggage posed no threat to the plane or its passengers.

5. *National explosives detection canine teams* are TSA officers paired with dogs that are trained to quickly locate and identify bombs and materials that could be used to manufacture explosives. These teams are deployed in some airports.

Not unexpectedly, TSA has two points of emphasis. The first is to prevent weapons of all types from being taken onto airplanes. The second is to deal more effectively with terrorists who do manage to board airplanes. Remember that the 9/11 terrorists used box cutters as weapons, and as a result, the TSA established a set of rules to govern the types of instruments that may and may not be packed in checked luggage or carried onto the plane. Checked luggage is typically x-rayed, but in smaller airports, it may be searched by TSA luggage screeners instead. Carry-on luggage is x-rayed at the same time passengers pass through a metal detector. If baggage screeners identify a suspicious item in either checked or carry-on luggage, that luggage is opened and searched by hand. Similarly, if an alarm sounds as the passenger passes through the metal detector, that person is asked to remove any metal objects from his or her pockets and walk through the metal detector again. If the alarm goes off a second time, the passenger may be scanned with a handheld metal detector or "patted down" by the screener.

When forbidden devices (such as tools more than 7 inches long or knives) are found, the passenger has the option to return to check-in, retrieve his or her luggage, and place the object in it. Typically the potential weapon is confiscated, and the passenger is allowed to continue through the screening process. Displays of confiscated objects ranging from hunting knives to martial arts weapons are available in some airports.

As noted elsewhere, in August 2006, authorities in the United Kingdom arrested a number of people who planned to carry and detonate bombs on as many as ten American airliners. This group of terrorists planned to use liquid- or gel-based bombs that would not be detected during the course of the screening process that was in place at that time. After those arrests, the TSA developed these guidelines regarding carrying liquids and gels onto commercial aircraft:

- Liquids and gels may be brought into the secure area so long as they are carried in a clear, one-quart plastic bag. Each passenger may carry only one such bag.

- Items to be placed in individual containers in the bag include but are not restricted to shampoo, creams, lotions, hair gel, and toothpaste.

- The capacity of individual containers may not exceed three ounces.

- Passengers who do not adhere to these guidelines may not pass through screening.

Here are the exceptions to these guidelines:

- *Baby formula, breast milk, and over-the-counter and prescription medications* may be in containers larger than three ounces and do not have to be carried in one-quart bags. However, they must be declared at the time the passenger enters the secure boarding area. (*Note:* Boarding passengers should be prepared to show these items to TSA officials.)

- *Solid cosmetics and personal hygiene items* such as tubes of lipstick may be taken onto the airplane without inspection.

- How effective is the TSA? The current security system is not perfect, but there have been no successful attacks on U.S. airplanes since 9/11. Nonetheless, steps are being taken to improve the system.

IMPROVING THE SYSTEM: SOME BARRIERS

Clearly the system that has been constructed by the TSA falls short of the one developed by El Al. Why does it fall short? The El Al system is expensive, and, as is the case with so many things in our society, neither the airline companies nor the federal government has stepped up with the resources needed. There is some evidence that passengers are willing to pay higher fares if safety is improved, but, generally speaking, airline company officials have been reluctant to test this theory. Even so, important efforts are under way to improve airline safety. I'll discuss some of these efforts at the end of this section.

A second barrier to the improvement of the security system at airports and on planes is public opinion. Racial profiling is an important tool in the fight against terrorism. In the 1960s and 1970s, most of the hijackings involved Cubans. Today the biggest concern is focused on Islamic terrorists. However, racial profiling raises many concerns among the citizenry of this country and is unlikely to become a part of the TSA's arsenal against terrorists.

One proposal that would tighten security has been placed on hold. The 9/11 Commission suggested that all foreign passengers boarding aircraft be digitally fingerprinted before being allowed on the plane, but airline company officials and the governments of some foreign countries have balked at this suggestion. Foreign governments are concerned that their citizens would be unfairly targeted. Airline company officials complain that it would impede the boarding process, which may be true. It is also likely that fingerprinting conducted by airline employees would require additional employees, but the airline industry is labor intensive, and industry officials are constantly searching for ways to eliminate personnel to cut costs. My guess is that the logistics of the boarding process could be handled if fingerprinting of foreign fliers is required, but the TSA seems to have acquiesced to the pressure applied by the airline industry and some foreign countries; fingerprinting is a dead issue… for now.

U.S. fliers hate to be inconvenienced. We have adjusted to arriving at airports 1–1.5 hours before our flights, but what would the reaction be to the El Al expectation that passengers arrive 3 hours before the flight and submit to a one-on-one interrogation before being allowed to check in? Not positive, would be my guess. Dozens of complaints have been lodged against TSA officials because of invasive screening procedures, the requirement that passengers remove body piercings, and what some term as "failure to use good judgment."

FIXING THE SYSTEM: EXPLOSIVES SCANNERS

After the rash of skyjackings involving people who wanted to leave or go to Cuba, metal detectors were installed in airports around the United States. The incidence of hijackings dropped dramatically. Not surprisingly, the TSA is turning to technology to decrease the threat of terrorism.

Two promising devices are being tested: the *walk-through explosive trace detection portal* and the *trace detection document scanner*. Walk-through portals are now in place in at least twenty-three airports, including those in Los Angeles, Chicago (ORD), New York (JFK), Dallas–Fort Worth, Boston, and Phoenix. The testing of document scanners has not continued apace. Document scanners are being tested at Los Angeles International, John F. Kennedy in New York, Ronald Reagan National Airport in Washington, DC, and Chicago's O'Hare airport. Additionally, a shoe-scanning device is being tested at LAX to determine its utility in the fight against terrorism. Additional deployment of the document- and shoe-scanning devices will be dependent on the test results and the availability of funds. At this juncture, it seems that the TSA is committed to deploy the walk-through portals as quickly as funding permits.

Currently two models of walk-through portals have been adopted as funds become available: General Electric's EntryScan3 and Smiths Detection's IONSCAN SENTINEL II. Both of these models pass air gently over the body to loosen minute particles that are then analyzed for the presence of explosives, drugs, and biological agents. The walk-through portals also produce an X-ray image of the passenger that allows the screeners monitoring the devices to identify weapons and other types of contraband. Both models of the walk-through portals are now in production and can be deployed quickly. Concerns about possible retention and dissemination of images have not slowed the deployment process. I have spoken to people who have been screened using walk-through portals and other than the fact that the burst of air that is supposed to loosen particles of contraband for analysis messes up your hair, they found the screening quick and unobtrusive.

The explosives trace detection document scanners now being tested were developed, as the name suggests, to detect the presence of explosives and other illegal substances on documents such as passports. Once documents are scanned, the device can detect the presence of forty different forms of explosives and narcotic substances. The analysis takes eight seconds to perform. This device, which is priced at $43,000, is also in production at this time and could be deployed quickly. Although neither of the test results were available at the time this book went to print, it seems likely that the portals and document scanners will soon be more widely used.

In the near future, emerging technology will also provide an additional degree of safety beyond that now provided by X-rays and screening by hand. For example, multiview X-ray equipment will substantially increase the ability of screeners to see and identify explosives, drugs, and other types of contraband. Additionally, the TSA has ongoing research and development projects designed to improve screening of containerized air cargo and mail. Fingerprint identification systems, facial recognition software, and iris recognition systems are now being tested, both to increase safety and to speed the process of screening pilots and other personnel as they move in and out of secure areas.

ARMING PILOTS

In the aftermath of 9/11, a number of pilots and others opined that the hijackings could have been prevented if the aircraft crews had been armed with pistols. A firestorm of debate followed, but in 2003, Congress agreed to arm those pilots who underwent extensive training. Guns in the cockpit raised additional safety issues, particularly in the minds of fearful fliers. For example, what would happen if a bullet penetrated the skin of the aircraft? There were a number of rebuttals to this concern, and many came from pilots and others familiar with the construction of modern aircraft. One is that in two instances, planes have suffered major problems and remained airworthy. The side door on a United Airlines 747 failed and a large hole developed in the side of the aircraft. However, if I had been presented with this issue by a fearful flier, I would have countered with the story of what occurred when the entire front portion of an Aloha Airlines B-737 peeled off in flight: the plane returned to Honolulu and landed safely. The only fatalities were flight attendants who were not wearing seat belts at the time the skin of the plane over the nose peeled off.

Coincidentally on March 22, 2008, a US Airways pilot discharged his weapon accidentally. The bullet penetrated the fuselage of an Airbus A319. The plane did not decompress or crash. However, the wisdom of allowing pilots and first officers to carry firearms was questioned as a result of that accidental shot. Here are some of the objections that have been raised to guns in the cockpit and responses to those objections:

- *Since 9/11, the cockpit doors have been strengthened and are now impenetrable. Pilots are therefore in no danger and would be able to continue the flight during a terrorist attack.* Response: This is not an accurate statement because a terrorist with a small string of adhesive explosive and an easily rigged detonator could blast open cockpit doors.

- *Pilots are not trained to use firearms, and accidental deaths could occur.* Response: Pilots would only be firing at terrorists who would presumably be at close range. Additionally, to qualify to carry a pistol, a pilot must receive training from TSA-approved sources.

- *In the case of a hijacking, the pilot's first priority should be to land the plane, not to fight terrorists.* Response: This statement is accurate and is airline policy. However, some pilots contend that a plane flying at 30,000 feet will take at least twenty minutes to land. The report of the Aloha Airlines flight suggests that it may be possible to land the plane in less than twenty minutes, but in many instances, it will take far longer than twenty minutes to land a plane that is under attack, regardless of its altitude. During that time, a pilot with a weapon could fend off attackers, while one without a gun could not.

- *TSA provides armed air marshals to protect planes from terrorists.* Response: That is true, but very few planes have air marshals on board.

One last note about guns in the cockpit: Regardless of the policy for flights within the United States, pilots of international flights will not be armed because governments of other countries will not permit U.S. pilots to bring weapons into other countries.

CHAPTER 8

Coping with Anticipatory Anxiety

You get a call from your boss who tells you that you have been selected to represent the company at a crucial meeting in Albuquerque next month, or your spouse comes home with a "wonderful" surprise: you're going to Paris to celebrate your anniversary. For most people, representing their company or traveling to Paris would generate excitement. If you are afraid to fly and you suffer from anticipatory anxiety, these announcements produce only one response: dread.

What is *anticipatory anxiety,* and who suffers from it? More important, how do you rid yourself of it? One very simple definition of anticipatory anxiety is that it is the fear of fear. You are not flying today, but you begin to think about the day you will fly and that scares you and you begin to worry.

Anticipatory anxiety begins with automatic, fearful thoughts such as, "I'll die if I fly." In brief, you begin to worry. This produces an emotional state that varies tremendously from individual to individual. For some, thinking about the flight ahead brings only mild anxiety characterized by some muscle tension, an occasional headache, inability to concentrate for short periods of time, and perhaps a little sleep loss. For others, anticipatory anxiety brings about some or all of the following symptoms: migraine headaches, severe intestinal distress, lower-back pain, extreme insomnia, irritability, and nightmares of horrible events during what is usually restful sleep.

Just as there is considerable variation in anticipatory anxiety symptoms, there are differences in when anticipatory anxiety begins. For example, in an extreme case, a French lawyer could not concentrate well enough to practice law if he had a flight scheduled within a year, and he invariably cancelled all his flights. For most people, anxiety about flying does not set in until a week or so before the flight. It usually begins with mild anxiety and then builds to intense anxiety the night before the flight. In addition to the symptoms listed above, this may result in emotional outbursts.

Unfortunately, anxiety about flying does not subside once you reach your initial destination. You may summon the courage to fly to an exotic spot only to find that you spend your vacation worrying about the return flight or looking for alternate ways to get home. While not everyone experiences anticipatory anxiety, if you do, you will understand why I call it the meanest part of the fear of flying. It doesn't just make you uncomfortable during the flight, which is often of short duration. Anticipatory anxiety makes you miserable for days…and sometimes weeks.

One of the odd things about anticipatory anxiety is that it does not necessarily go away when you fly without fear. Many fearful fliers seek treatment primarily because of their anticipatory anxiety. They often report, "Once they close the door, I'm okay," but even if they can fly in comfort, they still experience anticipatory anxiety. You should assume that your anticipatory anxiety has a life of its own and that it must be treated as a part of your recovery. If you do not deal with it, there is a good chance that sooner or later you will eventually avoid flying altogether because of the psychic pain it generates. If you experience mild anticipatory anxiety, you may be able to tolerate it and keep on flying, but why accept the discomfort?

You can defeat anticipatory anxiety using one of the strategies presented next. A discussion of which of the strategies may be best for you will follow a discussion of what not to do.

TO SUPPRESS OR NOT TO SUPPRESS

Suppression is (1) the process of diverting your thoughts about flying through tactics such as listening to music or engaging in diversionary and often pleasurable activities or (2) systematically "not owning" your fearful thoughts. When you are not thinking about or are unaware of your fearful thoughts, you have no anxiety and are more comfortable.

Because your comfort level goes up when you suppress, you begin to actively engage in various suppression approaches. The problem is this: suppression is not curative and often works only for very short periods of time.

To demonstrate how suppression is a losing battle, try this: Tell yourself not to think about solving an important problem that needs attention in the very near future. If you are like most people, it will be virtually impossible to put it out of your mind, and the harder you try to suppress the thought, the more often it occurs. If you are able to suppress thoughts about important problems, then you have developed a skill that is counterproductive to the task of overcoming irrational fear. You will need to work very hard not to suppress your scary thoughts about flying.

The techniques outlined in the next two sections of this chapter are based on the idea that you need to invite your fear into your thoughts and then deal with it. If you are one of those people who does not know what it is about flying that scares you, begin immediately to identify those things about air travel that scare you. Accurate identification of your scary thoughts will be essential to the process of eliminating your anticipatory anxiety as well as to dealing with your fear while you are on the plane.

STRATEGY ONE: WORRY TIME

Worry time is a paradoxical strategy that may not make sense to you because it involves prescribing the symptom you're trying to eradicate— worry. Don't be concerned if you do not fully understand the rationale underpinning worry time. The best minds in the mental health field are not sure why it works. The important thing for you to remember is that it does work!

Identify Your Fears

How do you use worry time? Start by identifying your fears. Make a complete list of the things that scare you about flying. If you are afraid of dying in an airplane crash and do not have related fears, such as having a panic attack, your list might appear as follows:

- Mechanics do not repair planes properly.

- Many airlines are flying old planes that are unsafe.

- The planes will fall apart in turbulence.

- The landing gear may not come down, and we will crash.

- If I die, my children will have no one to care for them.

If you fear heights, you might have the following list:

- Turbulence will cause the plane to fall.

- The plane is so flimsy, I'll fall through the floor.

- The feeling I get when the pilot announces that we are at 35,000 feet is unbearable.

- I'll be up in the air for two hours with nothing supporting me, and we will fall.

If you are claustrophobic, you might have the following list:

- It will be hot and uncomfortable in the jet bridge, and I won't have enough air.

- They will run out of air during the flight, and I will suffocate.

- I can breathe for one hour, which is the scheduled time, but there will probably be a delay and I'll suffocate.

If you have panic attacks, you might have a list like this:

- As soon as they close that door, I'm trapped.

- I'll have a panic attack and will go crazy because there is no place to go.

- I'll have a panic attack and break out the glass in the windows.

- I'll have a panic attack and make a complete fool of myself and be totally embarrassed.

Of course, your list will be made up of other fears, although it may contain some of the fears from two or three of the sample lists. The important thing is that you develop as complete a list as possible at this time. You can add to it later, and I encourage you to do so. Now identify the things that scare you about air travel.

My Fears About Air Travel

_____

_____

_____

_____

_____

_____

_____

_____

_____

Establish a Time to Worry

You now have a list of the things that frighten you most about air travel. The next step is to set aside two ten-minute periods each day, one in the morning and one in the early evening, to worry. I suggest that you use the time when you are preparing to go to work as your first worry time and then choose a time just after dinner for the second worry session. Do not choose a time for a worry session just before you are planning to sleep because if you worry properly, it will upset you. Because worry time is designed to put you in touch with your fear, it may disrupt your sleep. You need time to relax prior to sleeping, and that is why the early evening is best for most people. If you are not on a typical nine-to-five schedule (i.e., you work midnight to 8 A.M.), select a time soon after you awake for the worry session.

Rules for Worrying

I know from experience that some of you are beginning to ask yourselves, "Is he serious?" Absolutely. Worry time, like all effective techniques, has procedures and rules that must be followed if it is to be effective. The rules for worry sessions are as follows:

1. Worry in a place where you will not be overheard.

2. Worry aloud.

3. Worry into a mirror if possible.

4. Do not contradict yourself even if you believe you have said something infinitely foolish.

5. Avoid rational thinking and concentrate on getting your irrational beliefs out.

6. Worry for the entire ten minutes, even if you run out of anything to worry about in a minute or so.

7. Don't call yourself stupid before, during, or after the worry session.

8. Try to get in touch with the "hook" (dying, looking foolish, etc.) and thus the emotion associated with your fear.

9. Restrict worry sessions to your fears about flying.

10. Worry twice a day until the anxiety begins to subside and then reduce the worry sessions to once a day.

If you follow these rules you will look at your watch, note the time, and begin to worry aloud. If you have only one fear, then the entire session might be devoted to that fear, perhaps the common misconception that turbulence creates unsafe flying conditions and that the plane will crash as a result. Here is a sample worry session involving multiple fears:

- *I hate airplanes. They are so small and cramped, and people are packed into them like sheep. It gets so warm in them, and there is not enough air for all those people to breathe. I get that tight feeling in my chest every time I get on a plane. And they are constructed so poorly. In turbulence, the overhead luggage compartments shake and even come open. When you walk down the aisle, you can feel the floor flex, they are built so poorly. I feel like I'm going to fall through the floor every time I get up, so I don't go to the lavatory and I get so uncomfortable. Once I thought I was going to soil myself and now I think about that and think how embarrassing that would be. I'll never put myself in that situation again. Mostly though, it's the terror I feel because I know that any second I will die. I sit very quietly, listening to every sound and watching the flight attendants. They are taught to smile even in the worst conditions, but they would show fear if something was really wrong with the airplane.* [Recycle these fears if the worry session lasts less than ten minutes.]

What to Do Between Worry Sessions

Purchase a small notebook to carry with you between worry sessions so you can write down any worrisome thought you have about flying. While you may think that I am being facetious, I do not want you to forget your worrisome thoughts. If a *new* worrisome thought pops up between worry sessions, write it down. Also, by keeping a record of your scary thoughts, you may begin to get a clearer picture of what your primary fears about flying are.

After you have written the scary thought down, simply say to yourself, "I'll worry about that in my next worry session" and dismiss it. This works very much like the "to do" list-making that people are taught in time-management courses. If you record each worry in your notebook and have an established time to worry about it, the anxiety evoked by the worry should diminish over time. How will you know it's working? Before you begin worry time, answer the following questions:

- How many days before a scheduled flight do I begin to worry?

- What are the symptoms associated with my anticipatory anxiety? What is the intensity of anxiety as measured by SUDS (see chapter 4)? What are my physical symptoms? (Make a list of physical symptoms such as tense muscles, shallow breathing, racing heart, heart palpitations, dizziness, headaches, diarrhea, etc.)

- If sleeplessness is a problem, when does it begin?

Answers to these questions can provide a baseline against which you can judge your progress:

- *How long will it take?* It depends on two variables—the intensity of your anxiety and how intent you are about completing your worry sessions—and could take from a few weeks to several months. You should see some progress within four to six weeks if you follow the rules listed previously.

- *How will you know when to stop?* You will stop either when your anticipatory anxiety is gone or when worrying is tolerable. The French lawyer who could not practice law if he had a flight scheduled stopped worry time after his anticipatory anxiety was reduced to a very mild anxiety the night before a flight. Rachel stopped when she got tired of hearing herself worry about things that were totally irrational. You should stop when you reach your own comfort level.

Returning to Worry Time

Most people who overcome their anticipatory anxiety will not have relapses. However, some do, usually because they read or watch detailed accounts of plane accidents or encounter something during a flight that scares them. If this happens to you, begin worry time immediately.

STRATEGY TWO: DISPUTING IRRATIONAL BELIEFS

Several mental health professionals, including Aaron Beck (1975) and Albert Ellis (1994), have highlighted the fact that our fearful, anxiety producing thoughts are the result of irrational beliefs. Worry time is one approach to dealing with your irrational thoughts. Another approach is to systematically dispute each thought as it occurs. When you use this approach, you literally talk back to your fear. Almost all fearful fliers play mind games with their fear, even to the point of developing acronyms with the word "fear." As noted earlier, many fearful people understand that "FEAR" stands for "false evidence appearing real" when it comes to airplanes. However, using disputing statements involves teaching yourself a new, subvocal response to your fearful thoughts.

The Initial Steps

The first step in this process is much like beginning worry time: make a list of your irrational beliefs. The second step involves using information you trust to write rejoinders to the fearful thoughts. The key word in that sentence is "trust." As has been mentioned many times, most fearful fliers believe a lot of inaccurate information about flying and what will happen to them on a plane. If you do not trust the information you have, it will be of no value to you when you dispute the accurateness of your fearful thoughts.

Adding Emotion

At least two emotions are antithetical to fear and can be included in your disputing statements. *Humor* will make you happy and break the power of your fear. *Anger* directed at your fear (remember: never at yourself) focuses your attention, energizes you, and allows you to confront your fear with more confidence.

Every person has a different sense of humor. If you are going to use humor, you need to understand your own sense of humor and how to activate it. One way to activate your humor is to exaggerate the danger. For example, you might tell yourself that your plane is so dangerous, it is likely to fall out of the sky while it is taxiing and then produce a mental image of your plane "falling" through the runway as it taxis. Sometimes just stringing several absurd thoughts together can be humorous: "With my luck the plane is bound to crash. When I throw a penny into the air it lands on its side; I can't even get a head or a tail. My pilot is probably from the remnants of the Japanese kamikaze squads; he's so inept he crashed into a battleship and lived. This flight is so dangerous that when I get on board, the flight attendants will be wearing parachutes."

You may be able to think of other humorous thoughts that will break the tension produced by your fear. After you have broken the tension with humor, dispute your thoughts with accurate information.

Anger can probably be activated more easily than humor for most people because they have more experience with this emotion. Because anger is often associated with the use of expletives, inserting swear words into your disputing statements may be all you need to become angry at your fear. You may also need to consider what your fear has done to you. Perhaps it has cost you a job or a promotion, damaged an important relationship, or kept you from seeing the beauty of the world. If a person did that to you, you would be angry! Do not direct this anger inwardly and call yourself names. Aim it at the alien in your mind—your fear.

The following lists represent the irrational fears of many people who are afraid to fly and also illustrate how accurate information and antithetical emotions can be used to dispute those fears. If you use humor in your statements, make sure that it does not detract from the value of the information included in the statement. Try to identify my feeble attempts to inject humor into the "D" statements below.

PERSON WHO HAS PANIC ATTACKS

1. I'll have a panic attack and do something crazy if I fly.

   Disputing statement: I may have a panic attack, but I can control my [*expletive of your choosing*] response and I won't go crazy.

2. I'll have a panic attack and have a heart attack.

   D: I may have a panic attack, but my heart is healthy. Besides, if you are going to have a heart attack, a plane is the best place to be. The captain's responsibility is to get sick passengers the best care as quickly as possible.

3. I'll have a panic attack and be catatonic for the rest of my life.

   D: I won't become catatonic, but if I did, there would be no more exercise.

4. I'll take the train instead of the plane. At least if I have a panic attack, I can pull the emergency cord and get off.

    D: That's smart! You'll probably be in the middle of a Georgia swamp when you have the attack. You love snakes and alligators.

PERSON WHO IS CLAUSTROPHOBIC

1. If I fly, I'll run out of air and suffocate.

    D: Not likely: The air is changed in the plane at least once every ten minutes.

2. When they close the door, I'll panic and hyperventilate.

    D: No, I won't. I know exactly how to control my breathing using the RED technique.

3. It's so hot and stuffy in that jet bridge, I'll probably panic when I'm boarding the plane.

    D: I'll be smart. I'll check in and then board the plane at the last minute.

4. If we have a delay, I'll panic.

    D: Hell no, I won't panic. I can control my breathing.

5. The air is so stale in the plane, it will make me sick.

    D: No—the plane is filled with fresh air. We'll probably smell the stockyards when we land in Chicago.

PERSON WHO IS ACROPHOBIC

1. If we hit turbulence, the plane will fall.

    D: That's nonsense! No plane has ever been knocked out of the sky by turbulence.

or

    D: Sure—planes fall from the sky so often, you have to wear a hard hat to keep plane parts from hitting you in the head.

2. After takeoff, when the captain lowers the nose, the sinking feeling I get scares me and I may panic.

   D: Stop! That sensation is perfectly normal, and the plane isn't falling; it's climbing and accelerating.

3. The announcement that we have reached our cruising altitude of 35,000 feet scares me.

   D: Higher is safer. We are riding on solid columns of air, and the plane *cannot* fall.

PERSON WHO IS AEROPHOBIC

1. Most airlines are cutting corners because they are losing money.

   D: Stop! Airlines lose money when they have accidents.

2. We'll fly into a thunderstorm and die.

   D: Thunderstorms are dangerous, but the captain of the plane wants to get home just as much as I do.

3. If we get into clouds, we'll have a midair collision.

   D: Don't be silly! The ATC and TCA will prevent midair collisions.

4. Flying is unsafe, and I will die if I get on a plane.

   D: Planes are safer than automobiles.

5. I'll cancel my reservation and drive. I'm in control then.

   D: Stop it, you control freak. You are not in control of other drivers when you are in a car.

Moving on from these examples, it is time for you to write down your irrational fears and disputing statements in the space provided if you intend to use this strategy to deal with your anticipatory anxiety. As you write statements to dispute your fears, you may have to return to earlier chapters to get the information you need. In the column marked with a "T" (for "trust"), rate the extent to which you trust the information you have used in the disputing statement; use a 1–10 scale with a

1 meaning you do not trust the information at all and a 10 meaning that you almost completely trust the information that you have used. If the rating you give is below 5, it means that you should get additional details or information from more credible sources to increase your trust that the information you have is valid.

Disputing My Irrational Fears

My Fears	Disputing Statements	T
_____	_____	
_____	_____	___
_____	_____	
_____	_____	___
_____	_____	
_____	_____	___
_____	_____	
_____	_____	___
_____	_____	
_____	_____	___
_____	_____	
_____	_____	___
_____	_____	
_____	_____	___

Using Disputing Statements

After you have written statements that dispute your irrational fear, it is time to begin using them to overcome your anticipatory anxiety. These kinds of thoughts may occur at various times, so be ready for them. A physician wrecked his Mercedes when he became so distracted by his thoughts that he forgot he was on a busy street. The procedure for using the thoughts is as follows:

1. Memorize the responses. If you think you might forget them, write them on adhesive note pads and put them in a number of places such as the bathroom, the dash of your car, and around your work area.

2. Whenever a thought occurs, dispute it immediately.

3. Get angry!

WHICH TECHNIQUE SHOULD YOU USE?

My suggestion is that you choose either worry time or disputing irrational thoughts, depending entirely on which one seems most attractive to you. Some fearful fliers use a combination of the two, that is, they use worry time twice a day and then dispute irrational thoughts between worry times. My concern about this approach is that you may overload yourself and stop using either strategy. So to begin, select one technique and use it!

Are There Other Things You Can Do?

In addition to worry time or disputing irrational thoughts, there are three other things you can do:

1. Use the RED technique and control your breathing for five to seven minutes whenever your anxiety gets unbearable. This will be particularly important if your anticipatory anxiety keeps you awake.

2. Once you have slowed your breathing, scan your body and find tense muscles. Relax them by the Identify-Tense-Relax (ITR) method.

3. Consider medication if your anxiety becomes intense. The exact type of medication will need to be determined by your physician, but Valium (diazepam), Xanax (alprazolam), Klonopin (clonazepam), and Ativan (lorazepam) are some of the drugs often prescribed for this problem. I will tell you because some physicians do not: these drugs are addictive. If you have had problems with addictions (e.g., alcoholism), you may want to work especially hard to use the other strategies described here before using drugs. Also, because these medications are addictive, if you take them regularly for anticipatory anxiety, you will need to withdraw from them slowly, probably over a period of weeks.

PREFLIGHT PLANNING

This section outlines the process of planning for the flight to help those people who have not flown recently develop an awareness of the steps that they must take when they decide to return to flying or take their first flight. Encountering the unexpected as you make your reservation, travel to the airport, and pass through check-in and screening can arouse unnecessary anxiety and increase the probability that you will not board your flight. The information you get in this section will be put to work in chapter 9 as you make imaginary trips to the airport, airplane boardings, and flights.

Making a Reservation—Decisions, Decisions

Before you make your reservation, lay out a master plan that involves flying several times, if at all possible. Once you have taken your first flight, you need to fly again, preferably within three months, and sooner is better. All too often I have seen people who did not fly within a few months of their first successful flight begin to doubt their ability to be successful again and have their fear return. Don't let this happen to you.

I want you to be in control of every step in the preparation for your next flight, and this includes making the reservation. Decide on the length of flight you wish to take, and whether the flight is to be for business or pleasure. I recommend that you schedule the flight for the business of facing your fear of flying and the pleasure of leaving that fear behind. I believe that your only objective on your graduation flight should be to work on eliminating your fear of flying. If it is a business trip or a family vacation, other issues, such as keeping up appearances in front of colleagues or watching your children, may keep you from concentrating on your fear.

I recommend that your flight be of short duration, by which I mean forty-five minutes to an hour in the air. If you live on either the East or West coasts, there are numerous flights available to you that are of relatively short duration. Many airlines offer shuttle services, such as those between New York and Boston or Los Angeles and San Francisco. These flights may take off every hour or so, and they last from forty-five to sixty minutes. You could, for example, fly in the morning to Boston or San Francisco for lunch and return that same afternoon.

Published airline schedules give the time from gate to gate. A flight that is scheduled to depart at 1 P.M. and arrive at 2 P.M. will be in the air about forty-five minutes. The remainder of the time will be spent backing away from the jet bridge, taxiing, or waiting. The reason why I recommend that you take a short flight is because they have one distinct advantage: if you cannot reboard the plane, you can always rent a car or take the train back to your point of origin. More than three thousand fliers boarded our graduation flights when the American Airlines program for fearful fliers was operating. Only two elected not to take the return flight, but almost all fearful fliers who boarded those flights had some fear that they would be unable to make the return trip. If you schedule a short flight, the fear of being unable to get back on the plane is minimized. Other advantages of short flights are cost and not needing to take luggage. Also, if you schedule your flight on Saturday, there will likely be less traffic congestion in the parking areas, fewer people in the airport, and fewer people on the plane because in many areas fewer people fly on Saturday than any other day. Flights on Sunday afternoon, Monday morning, and Friday afternoon are likely to be crowded because these are peak travel periods.

In addition to deciding whether to take a short, intermediate, or long flight, you should also consider whether you wish to fly during the day or night. Some fearful fliers prefer to fly during the day so they can watch the ground. Others prefer flying at night because the darkness makes them less aware of the height of the airplane. From a safety viewpoint, it makes no difference whether you fly at night or during the day. If you have some concerns about the time of day you fly, take those concerns into consideration on this flight. However, your goal should be to fly comfortably during the night or the day.

You should also decide whether you wish to fly a narrow-body (one-aisle) or wide-body (two-aisle) aircraft. People with claustrophobia almost always prefer to fly a wide-body because they are much more spacious. Some people who have had or are having panic attacks also prefer a wide-body because they can get up and move about during the flight. Also, because turbulence is a bit less noticeable on large planes, some fearful fliers who are particularly concerned about this issue prefer a wide-body. If you take my recommendation and take a short flight, you will have few choices about the type of plane you fly. If you are flying across the United States or to the Caribbean, Mexico, or Canada, you may have options. If you book your flight online, at the time you select your seats, you will be shown the plane that will be used on your flight. If you book with an agent, ask about the equipment. One last note: if you have panic attacks, you may wish to select a regional jet because of the number of people on the plane. This a small plane, but it takes less time to board and deplane and may not involve a jet bridge. A typical narrow-body commercial aircraft seats 130 to 150; the seating capacity of regional jets is typically less than 65.

Do you want to fly first class or coach? The cabins of many aircrafts are divided into a section for each of these classes. Some wide-body planes have a third section, business class. First class is more expensive, costing two to eight times the coach-class fare depending upon the length of the trip. Business class is roomier than coach and costs two to four times as much as coach class in some instances; seats are wider and more comfortable, and you will receive better service. Both first and business class are in the front of the airplane and are quieter. Many people with claustrophobia can fly in moderate comfort in first and business class because of the extra space. They, and people who have had or now have panic attacks, feel less "trapped" in business and first class. You must decide if the extra money is worth the extra comfort. You should also be thinking long term. Will you normally be flying in coach class in the future? If so, you should probably be flying in coach class on your graduation flight.

What seat should you choose? Typically airplanes have aisle, middle, and window seats in the coach-class area. Most people who suffer from claustrophobia or who have panic attacks prefer aisle seats because they feel less confined. In a bit of a paradox, some people who are claustrophobic prefer to sit by the window and look out because this gives them the illusion of having more space. If you are claustrophobic and have the opportunity to board a stationary plane, try both aisle and window seats to see which one works best for you.

I recommend that you take a window seat if you are afraid of heights and are not claustrophobic. If you are sitting by the window, you can lower the plastic shade and thus control your visual space. Probably the second-best place for you to sit if you are afraid of heights is on the aisle. The objective is to not look out until the plane starts its descent. Then and only then should you look out of the plane, and this should not occur until you hear the clunk of landing gear being locked into place. Finally, if you have a choice between sitting in the tail of the coach-class section or toward the front, choose the front, particularly if you are concerned about turbulence, are worried about the noises in the aircraft, or are claustrophobic. Remember, the most stable portion of the plane is over the wings. However, the middle of the plane is also one of the noisiest sections because much of the machinery that controls the surface of the wings and the landing gear is located under the wing area.

The tail of the plane tends to move a bit more than the more stable portions of the plane and to bounce a bit more in turbulence. Also, when you are seated in the rear of the plane, you will usually be able to hear changes in engine noise as the pilot uses the throttle to increase or decrease the speed of the aircraft. These changes in noise level can be quite disconcerting. It may help you to recall how it sounds when you change the speed of your car as you travel across town or across country. Before the day of the flight, make several practice trips to the airport, particularly if you are concerned about driving or being trapped in crowded places. Make sure that you know where to park and where to check your baggage (if you will have baggage with you). There are usually three places where you can park: short-term, long-term, and off-site lots. Typically, the cost of parking is directly related to proximity to the airport. At some airports, short-term parking can cost $30 per day or more. Some fearful fliers who have not planned ahead have accidentally parked in short-term parking only to find after they return from their trips that parking cost more than their airline tickets.

Things to Take

You now know that the pilot and dispatcher plan each flight carefully. You should also plan your flight, particularly if you have medical problems such as hypoglycemia (low blood sugar) or motion sickness. On most flights, no meals will be served, although snacks in the form of peanuts, crackers, or cookies may be made available. Make sure you pack whatever food is needed to control your condition in your carry-on luggage. I also recommend that you pack a few light snacks and that you purchase a bottle of water once you have cleared security. The security screeners will confiscate water and other liquids if you bring them from home.

Motion sickness is another issue that should be anticipated. It occurs because the inner ear sends faulty information to the brain. If you have motion sickness, you may use over-the-counter products such as Dramamine (dimenhydrinate) and Bonine (meclizine). However, my recommendation is that you contact your physician several days before your flight and get a prescription for much more effective remedies such as Antivert (meclizine) or Valium (diazepam). As you know by now, Valium is addictive and therefore it should only be used as a last resort. However, if Valium is the only means available to you to control your motion sickness, restrict its use to the time just before the flight.

Nasal congestion also needs to be taken into consideration as you plan your flight. If you are mildly congested, you can fly if you use decongestant pills or nasal sprays. Use the latter if you have high blood pressure, because many decongestants raise your blood pressure. Alternatively, ask your pharmacist for a decongestant other than pseudoephedrine (which raises your blood pressure, elevates your heart rate, and may increase your nervousness). Do not fly if you are severely congested because you may damage your inner ear. If there is any question about the extent of your congestion and the potentially damaging effects of compression and decompression, contact your physician.

Another aspect of preflight planning is the compilation of a list of clothing and personal items you wish to take on your trip. Trying to remember what you need just before the flight may be difficult—remember, the brain doesn't function in the usual way when you are fearful or anxious—so making a list can be key. Whether you are taking luggage or not on your trip, you should pack the following items for your graduation flight:

- A small bottle of drinking water or juice for a dry mouth (purchased after you pass through security; no caffeinated drinks)

- Some tissues for sweaty palms

- Nasal spray or decongestant if you are congested (small: 0.5 ounce)

- Headache remedy of choice

- Any medicines you are taking regularly, in case you are delayed

- A sweater or jacket in case the pilot turns the air-conditioning too high (summer and winter)

- An MP3 or CD player if you intend to dance to the turbulence

- Crossword puzzles or a magazine to entertain you if you get bored (it is possible!)

- Chewing gum to help relieve tension in the ears (chewing gum causes you to swallow more; swallowing tends to equalize the internal and external pressure and eliminate the discomfort that can result when the plane ascends or descends)

- Lens rewetting solution if you wear contacts

- Clothing

The Day Before the Flight

If you plan to take a taxi or limousine, call a day ahead to schedule the service and verify that the car will come on the day of the flight. The last thing you want is to miss your flight because of transportation problems, although you may have different thoughts about this at this time.

If your carrier allows, check in online twenty-four hours before the flight and print your boarding passes at home. Online check-in typically allows you to enter the number of bags that you will be checking. You should have been told at the time you made your reservation how many bags you could check (typically one or two) and the maximum weight of each bag (typically 50 pounds) before extra charges are imposed. If not, call your carrier to get the information you need. Weigh your bags once they are packed and, if they are overweight, unpack some of the contents or prepare to pay a fee.

Time to Go to the Airport

The day of your flight has arrived. Your first impulse may very well be to call in sick...sick of flying. You may also have some flu-like symptoms such as headache, upset stomach, and diarrhea. Don't make that call. Remember, avoidance makes the problem worse. If you have several hours to spend prior to your departure to the airport, keep busy with meaningful tasks. Exercise if possible. It burns off the excess epinephrine that your body is generating and keeps the oxygen in your bloodstream at a normal level.

The rule for preparing for the trip to the airport and getting to the plane after you arrive is to avoid surprises. But one such surprise can be out of your control—delays. Before you leave home, contact the airline to verify that your flight departure is on time. It will add to your anxiety to arrive at the airport and find that your flight has been delayed.

As mentioned earlier, decide in advance how you will get to the airport, how long the trip will take, and when you need to arrive to check in. The typical recommendation is that you arrive 1–1.5 hours before the flight for domestic flights and a bit earlier for international flights.

You will need a government-issued picture identification document (driver's license or passport) to check in. If you have completed an online check-in, all you need to do is go to the curbside check-in (if it is available), check your bags, and head for security. If you have not checked in online and there is no curbside check-in available, proceed to the check-in counter of your airline or to the kiosks. Airlines have introduced *kiosks* (computerized self–check-in stations) as one means of reducing personnel costs. To use the kiosk, you will need one or two other forms of identification: your frequent-flier card and the credit card you used to pay for your ticket when you made the reservation. (The one thing that fearful fliers want least is a frequent-flier card, but make sure you have one before you go to the airport if at all possible.)

Kiosks walk you through check-in with touch screens. The first step is to insert either your credit card or frequent-flier card. The next screen displays your itinerary and asks if you are checking luggage. If the answer is yes, an agent will check your picture identification and help you with your bags. Whether the answer is yes or no, the kiosk will print your boarding passes and you will be on your way to security.

Your boarding pass and picture identification will be checked as you enter security. You will not need your government-issued picture identification again, but you will need to present your boarding pass to the TSA screeners in order to pass through security. As you approach the walk-through metal detectors, you are asked to place all metallic objects in trays along with your shoes, jackets, and, in some cases, hats. As was mentioned earlier, screeners may ask that you remove body-piercing jewelry and place these items in trays as well. Electronic devices such as cell phones, cameras, and computers must also be placed in trays. All of your personal belongings are then x-rayed while you walk through the metal detector.

Once you are screened, you are free to proceed to the area where your flight is boarding. As you wait, you will hear periodic messages not to leave baggage unattended and to report suspicious behavior to TSA officials. This makes some people nervous, but think of it as a reminder that they need to take personal responsibility for their own safety.

Every airline has a unique system for boarding passengers. But typically you can prepare to meet the pilot of your flight as you walk down the jet bridge to your plane. The pilot and first officer will be in the flight deck busy preparing for your flight. Some fearful fliers simply want to say hello; others want to look the pilot in the eye or smell his or her breath. That is inappropriate. Pilots are professionals and if you are not too intrusive, they will welcome you. Once you enter the aircraft, you need to quickly find your seat and place your carry-on luggage in the overhead compartments or under the seat in front of yours. If you have problems, consult one of the flight attendants.

When the time for the flight to take off arrives, the doors of the plane will be closed and secured. Once the plane is pressurized, the doors cannot be reopened until after the plane lands. There are times both before takeoff and after landing that delays of varying lengths occur. Some delays have lasted for several hours, and passengers have not been allowed to deplane. Typically these delays are attributable to weather, either at the point of departure or at the destination.

Passengers want to know why their planes do not return to the terminals and why they are not allowed to deplane when lengthy delays occur. Sometimes there are no gates for the planes at the terminals. This is a legitimate reason for keeping people on planes for extended periods of time, but it is rarely the case that some accommodation could not be made. More likely the reason for not returning to the airport is that airplanes are in a queue waiting for departure. If a plane returns to the terminal, it loses its place in line and further delays the flight. This is one of those times when passenger comfort is sacrificed for schedule.

CHAPTER 9

Coping on the Plane

The ultimate test in your fight to conquer your fear of flying is to cope with your fear while you are actually flying. This chapter is a dress rehearsal for your first successful flight. As you read this chapter, try to project yourself into the action, that is, imagine yourself doing each of the activities that are described and doing them with confidence. In chapter 8, I addressed preflight planning. In chapter 10, you will be asked to prepare a specific flight plan that addresses your fears. This chapter is a rehearsal for the real thing, but the rehearsal will necessarily be in your imagination.

FIND THE BOARDING AREA

Make certain that you are available to board your flight thirty minutes prior to departure. You should have a boarding pass, but in the event that you do not, check in with the gate agent. Examine your boarding pass and have it ready when your zone, row, or seat identifier (some airlines use letters; others use numbers) for boarding the aircraft is called. At this point, put your watch away and begin to attend only to your body. Many fearful fliers exacerbate their fear by continuously looking at their watches hoping that time is racing by. Of course, you know what happens: The watch seems not to move at all. Put it away, but in a place where you can find it easily. You may need it later on the plane.

It is a wise move for some fearful fliers to board the plane at the last possible minute but no later than ten minutes before the flight is scheduled to depart. For example, if you are claustrophobic or have panic attacks, you should board the plane at the last minute for two reasons. First, if you board with the other passengers, you are likely to find yourself packed into the jet bridge with a great many other people. This activates the fear of being trapped. Additionally, in the summertime the jet bridge can be extremely warm, a condition that also activates fear of suffocation in many claustrophobics. Second, if you delay boarding the plane until the final boarding period, you can keep moving, which may help lower your anxiety level.

When you do board the plane, go to your seat and make yourself as comfortable as possible. Make sure that you have your rubber band around your hand and directions for the RED technique where you can consult them easily. Leave nothing to your memory. You cannot remember facts when you are frightened. Once you are seated and your seat belt is securely fastened, check your SUDS score (1–10) and begin to control your breathing using the RED technique. After five minutes, check your SUDS score again to see if you are making any progress. Continue to control your breathing until you are well into the flight. If you cannot control your breathing, relax the muscles involved in the breathing process by using the Identify-Tense-Relax method. If your heart is racing, you may also wish to use the Valsalva maneuver in conjunction with your breathing. You will construct a flight plan for yourself in the next chapter. However, controlling your breathing will be a part of all flight plans.

If you begin to have those scary, intrusive thoughts, use your rubber band with a vengeance. If it is properly placed over the palm of your hand, you cannot injure yourself. Use this "weapon" as often as you need to and accompany it with orders to yourself (injunctions) to *stop* thinking those scary thoughts and with "I can" reminders that you are a strong person who can cope with your fear.

When you board the plane in the summertime, the air coming into the plane is air-conditioned. If humid conditions exist, you may see a gray vapor coming from the vents located just above your head along both sides of the plane. Many travelers have mistaken this vapor for smoke. It is not smoke. It is condensation from the air-conditioning unit. The way to tell condensation from smoke is that condensation dissipates; smoke does not. Smoke stays in the air and becomes progressively thicker.

Next, locate the card that is in the seatback pocket in front of you that tells you the type of plane you are flying. This will be useful later as you try to identify the sounds the plane makes.

Five minutes prior to departure from the gate you will hear a single chime when the captain illuminates the fasten–seat-belt sign. Soon after the chime, a flight attendant will ask you to fasten your seat belt.

THE FLIGHT

The flight will begin with an announcement from the ground crew thanking you for flying their airline. The door will then be shut and locked into place, and you will hear the announcement, "Flight attendants, please prepare for departure," and a single chime. The shutting of the door is a difficult time for many fearful fliers because they feel that they cannot get off the plane once the door is locked. If this is a difficult time for you, do not sit and listen intently for the signal that the door is about to close. Work on your breathing and try to keep yourself as calm as possible. Remind yourself that you chose to be on this flight because you know that you *can* handle air travel.

The announcement that the plane is about to depart lets the flight attendants know that the plane is about to leave the jet bridge and is an instruction to them to arm the evacuation slides so that the slides will deploy automatically if an emergency evacuation is required.

Departure and Engine Start

Typically the plane is pushed back from the gate by a heavy tug. Once the plane is in the taxiway, the engines are started and the plane is ready to taxi to the runway. In the event you are flying a commuter and you did not board the plane using a jet bridge, the pilot will simply start the engines and begin to taxi to the runway.

The process of starting a jet engine is unique, particularly on larger planes. The captain diverts air from a small jet engine called an *auxiliary power unit* (APU) to start the main jet engines. Until start time, the APU has probably been used to provide air-conditioning or heating and electricity to the plane. When engine start begins, you will notice the lights flicker because the power is interrupted momentarily. This may occur two or three times depending on how many engines your plane has. This is perfectly normal and does not mean that there is a short in the electrical system.

When the air is diverted from the air-conditioning system to the starter, the air that has been coming into the plane through the small vents (sometimes called *gaspers* or *eyeball vents*) and the swishing sound it makes will stop. Fresh air is still coming into the plane but at a greatly reduced rate. Although this slowing of fresh air only lasts for two or three minutes, on a hot, muggy day, the temperature inside the plane may rise a bit. If you are claustrophobic, the noticeable reduction of air flow and the rising temperature may activate your fear. Anticipate this event, remind yourself that fresh air is still coming into the plane, and concentrate on controlling your breathing.

Taxi Out

Once the jet engines have begun and permission to taxi has been received by the pilot from ground control, the captain will begin to taxi. As you taxi toward the runway, four things will occur that may frighten you. One of these is that you will smell the acrid exhaust from other airplanes. The plane is not on fire! Planes take air in from outside; if your plane is directly behind another plane, you will get some of its exhaust. Rest assured that the captain smells the fumes just as you do and will eliminate the problem as quickly as possible.

You will also hear grating and sometimes chattering from the huge disc brakes as the captain slows and stops during taxiing. While this awful sound would mean disaster if it occurred in your car, it is perfectly normal for airplanes. Incidentally, this sound would be much worse if your plane landed a few minutes prior to departure and the brakes had not had a chance to cool.

During taxi the flight attendants make the safety announcements telling you how to fasten and unfasten your seat belt, where the emergency exits are located, what to do with the oxygen mask in the case of depressurization, and about the flotation devices you will need if the plane makes a landing in water. They make this announcement on each flight because it is the law. You should pay close attention to these announcements, particularly those dealing with the emergency exits. The chances are extremely slight that you will ever have to use them, but if you do, you want to know where they are. The flight attendants are trained to empty a full plane in ninety seconds, even with half the exits blocked. You need to be ready to help by getting out of the plane if the need arises.

The pilot will extend the flaps on the wings on most planes during taxi. Two mechanical systems are used to deploy the flaps: either hydraulic pumps and jackscrews or cables. Boeing-built planes such as the B-767 typically have jackscrews that are driven by hydraulic pumps. When the flaps are deployed in Boeing-built planes, there is a high-pitched whine and a very noticeable mechanical sound of the jackscrews turning. The cable system, which is used in all planes built by Airbus, is much quieter, and if you are sitting away from the wing, you may not hear the flaps being deployed. However, if you are sitting near the wing, you will hear what sounds like a muffled groan when the flaps are deployed. You need to be able to identify these sounds because you will hear them during taxi, after takeoff, during climb, several times during descent, and after you land.

Please note that some planes do not deploy flaps prior to takeoff because the wing is so efficient it does not need the extra lift provided by flaps in many instances. The Fokker 100, a plane built in the Netherlands, is an example of such a plane. Don't panic if you do not see the flaps being extended on the wing of your aircraft.

One unpleasant and unexpected event that may occur just before takeoff is a ground delay. This occurs because air traffic control (ATC) at your destination has determined that they must slow incoming traffic to avoid holding patterns. Ask yourself this question, "Would I rather hold on the ground before takeoff or in the air before I land?" Almost all fearful fliers would rather hold on the ground.

Holding, whether it is in the air or on the ground, is a problem for all fliers, but people who are claustrophobic have the most trouble because they psych themselves up to take the flight, look at the scheduled flight time, and convince themselves that they can indeed breathe for one hour, albeit with difficulty. Then they get on the plane, taxi out, and hear this announcement, "Ladies and gentlemen, we have been advised that we will be held on the ground for thirty minutes because of weather in the Dallas area." Suddenly, the one-hour flight is one-and-a-half hours, and panic sets in. In one of the fearful flier seminars that I conducted, this exact scenario developed. Soon after the announcement, one of the participants jumped up and ran from her coach-class seat to first class, which is roomier. In about two minutes, she returned to her seat and started to work on controlling her breathing. She realized that if she could breathe for one hour, she could breathe for two or more hours. She changed her irrational thoughts.

Takeoff Roll

The takeoff begins with an announcement, "Flight attendants, prepare for takeoff," and a single chime. Once this is done, the captain may make either what is called a *rolling takeoff*, which means that the plane does not stop after it moves onto the runway, or a *standing takeoff*. Sometimes when a standing takeoff is used, the captain will set the brakes of the plane, allow the engine to rev up, and then release the brakes. This will usually occur on short runways (this does not mean they are dangerous) when the plane is fully loaded. If you are flying out of LaGuardia (New York City), Orange County's John Wayne Airport (Santa Ana, California), or St. Thomas (Virgin Islands), you are likely to experience this type of takeoff. It is also used on very hot days in some locations to ensure that the engines are generating maximum thrust at liftoff. Wings produce less lift in hot air and thus, because speed is one factor that influences lift, attaining maximum speed is essential to ensure needed lift. This may make more sense when you consider that it takes a jet engine six to seven seconds to reach its maximum power and the captain has decided to allow this to occur prior to the takeoff roll to ensure a safe takeoff.

Most takeoffs are standing takeoffs that involve nothing more than the captain slowly pushing the throttles forward to takeoff power and the plane moving ahead slowly at first, then accelerating faster and faster until it reaches the takeoff speed, which is in the neighborhood of 150 miles per hour for most planes. During this takeoff roll, you may hear a bump-bump-bump-bump as the nose wheel of the plane passes over the lights that are embedded in the center of the runway. Generally speaking, the captain will steer the plane to the left or right of these lights, and this noise will not last more than a few seconds. You may also feel some substantial bumps as the plane passes over expansion joints or rough places in the runway. These are not safety problems any more than they are when your car passes over expansion joints or bumps on the highways.

How long will the takeoff roll take? That depends upon the type of plane, the weather conditions, and the load. However, I have timed many small jets and commuters, and the usual takeoff roll is approximately thirty-five seconds. A B-757, which has the highest power-to-weight ratio of any commercial plane, may take only twenty-five seconds to complete the takeoff roll. A fully loaded B-747-400, which may weigh nearly 1,000,000 pounds when fully loaded, may take twice as long, or over a minute, to get to the speed it needs to fly.

Liftoff

The captain knows the exact speed needed for the plane to fly. This speed is precalculated based on the weight of the airplane, passengers, baggage, and weather conditions. So that this speed can be recognized easily, the captain places a small marker, known as a *bug*, on the airspeed indicator. Once bug speed is reached, the captain pulls back on the yoke, the nose lifts, and the plane begins to fly. For most people, this is the scariest moment in the flight. If this is your fear, you must work very hard to control your breathing and your heart rate. If racing thoughts occur, you should be ready to snap your rubber band and tell yourself to stop thinking those irrational thoughts. Snap the rubber band repeatedly and with vigor, if necessary. Then return immediately to controlling your breathing.

At the moment of liftoff, you will hear a thud as the weight is lifted from the landing gear. This occurs because the landing gear extends to its full limit in its housing. Within seconds, this sound will be followed by the landing-gear doors opening (thump), the landing gear coming up and being locked into place (bump), and the landing-gear doors closing (thump). This is a very noisy time and can be quite disconcerting if you do not anticipate these sounds and identify them as they occur.

If you are sitting in the rear of the plane at the time of *rotation* (when the captain pulls back on the yoke to raise the nose and lift off), you may experience the sensation that the plane is falling. This is not the case, but if you are in the rear of the plane you are actually descending for a split second. Why does it feel like this? At the time the nose of the plane comes up, the tail of the plane comes down several feet, and this is the source of the sinking feeling. Childhood teeter-totters produce the same feeling. Conversely, if you are sitting in the front of the plane at the time of rotation, you will have the sensation of rising, which you are. To help you visualize this experience, think of the plane as the teeter-totter or seesaw that you played on as a child. When one end goes up, the other end goes down.

Climb

The first thing you will hear during the climb is the sound of the flaps being retracted. This will typically occur in three stages as the plane accelerates. Listen for these sounds and, if you are sitting by a window and are not afraid of heights, verify that these are the sounds of the flaps by watching them move while the sound is occurring.

During the takeoff roll and at liftoff, the plane is at takeoff power. This is not unlike the situation you experience in your automobile when you are trying to get up enough speed to merge with traffic on the freeway. As soon as you get into the traffic pattern, you lift your foot off the accelerator. A few seconds into the climb, the captain reduces the power to *climb power* and lowers the nose of the aircraft to reduce the climb rate. This is done because the speed limit for an airplane below 10,000 feet is 281 miles per hour. If this is exceeded, the captain can be fined $10,000 or more. Slowing the climb rate also reduces engine wear and saves an airline money in maintenance costs. However, for many people, this combination of actions produces the sensation of falling.

Why does your body tell you that you are falling when you are in fact still climbing and accelerating? First, the noise in the airplane lessens, something you have always associated with slowing down. Second, because the nose is lowered, your stomach continues to climb for a split second, much the same as it does when you go over a large incline on a roller coaster. The difference is that on the roller coaster, you do in fact descend. In a plane, your mind interprets what is happening to you incorrectly: in effect, it lies to you. When pilots are in training, they are taught to ignore their senses and the mind's interpretation of what is occurring in the plane and to trust their instruments. Unfortunately, your seat is not equipped with an airspeed indicator and an altimeter.

You need to anticipate this first power reduction and the lowering of the nose and label it as it occurs by reminding yourself that the plane is not falling.

You may experience one or more turns soon after the plane lifts off. These are often necessary because of noise-abatement restrictions. I'm sure you can appreciate the fact that homeowners do not want planes flying over their houses at low altitudes, so, to accommodate them, planes are routed around populated areas. Planes turn when the captain simultaneously lowers one wing and raises the other using the *ailerons,* which are control surfaces hinged on the back of the wings near the wingtips (Conway and Tizzard 2008). When the plane banks, many people feel as though it is going to keep on rolling and fall out of the sky. Some feel this so intensely that they lean to the right if the plane is banking to the left to "help" the plane remain stable. The plane is quite stable, and your body movements are unnecessary. Banking turns are restricted to 30 degrees and under normal operating conditions will be no greater than this. However, it may help you to know that the plane could in fact make a 360-degree roll (all the way around), level off, and still fly quite nicely.

During the climb, you may also experience intermediate level-offs, which may surprise you. These occur primarily in areas of heavy traffic such as the New York/Newark, Dallas/Fort Worth, Chicago, Atlanta, Miami, and Los Angeles areas, but they can occur at any airport. You need to know that planes fly in highways in the sky just as you follow highways on the ground. These highways are spaced 1,000 feet apart vertically, and level-offs are necessary to maintain the 1,000 feet of separation required for planes that are flying under 10,000 feet.

When a level-off occurs, the captain lowers the nose of the aircraft and pulls the throttle back. This produces sensations that are not unlike those associated with the reduction of power from takeoff to climb, but they are less pronounced. However, many fearful fliers interpret these level-offs as signs that something is wrong with the aircraft. This is not the case. They are normal procedures.

WHAT THE CHIMES MEAN

Each airline decides how pilots and flight attendants will communicate, and thus chimes may have different meanings depending on the airline. The explanation that follows is the one used by American Airlines. I have already alerted you to the fact that you will hear a single chime at departure and another at takeoff. In both instances these are signals from the flight deck to the flight attendants and are typically accompanied by verbal announcements by the flight attendants. During the climb you will hear at least two chimes. One occurs at 1,500 feet to alert the flight attendants that they can begin their service. The second occurs at 10,000 feet. This alerts the flight attendant to announce that passengers may begin using devices (personal computers, tape players, CD players, etc.) that may interfere with navigational instruments and endanger the flight at lower altitudes. When the plane descends, the captain will once again ring a chime at 10,000 feet (flight attendants will ask passengers to stow restricted devices) and at 1,500 feet. You may hear other chimes during the climb as passengers request assistance by pushing the flight-attendant call button that is located either in the panel just above their heads or in their armrests.

By now you have determined that the chimes are a communication system between the pilots and the flight attendants, and between the passengers and the flight attendants. They also allow flight attendants in the front of the plane to communicate with those in the rear of the plane. When a chime sounds, flight attendants can recognize the source of the message by the color of a light that is illuminated in panels at both ends of the plane and thus they can distinguish whether it comes from a passenger, another flight attendant, or from the captain.

Unless the chimes are associated with the events already described, such as departure, takeoff, or passing 1,500 and 10,000 feet, they can be interpreted as follows:

One chime	Call me when you have time.
Two chimes	Call me as quickly as possible. (This allows the flight attendant to finish a task.)
Three chimes	Call me without delay.
Four chimes	Come to the cockpit now.

Four chimes are rarely heard and are used when something unusual is happening in the airplane. I was flying from Seattle to Raleigh-Durham when I heard four chimes: a drunken man had fallen, cut his head badly, and was beginning to bleed profusely. Immediately thereafter, there was an announcement asking if there was a physician on board. One was located, the passenger was cared for, and we proceeded to our destination. Four chimes would be used in the case of an emergency, and that is why you will hear it so rarely. I spoke personally with more than a dozen pilots who collectively have more than two hundred years of flying experience, and not one of them had ever used four chimes. There is a time when you might hear four or more chimes, however: children often discover the flight attendant call buttons in the armrests and may ring them repeatedly.

Cruise

An announcement such as, "Ladies and gentlemen, we have reached our cruising altitude of 35,000 feet and we are expecting smooth air, so I will be turning the seat-belt sign off at this time. Feel free to move about the cabin, but when you are in your seats, please keep your seat belts fastened for your safety," will alert you to the fact that you have reached your cruising altitude. You should comply with the request to keep your seat belt fastened because, as you now know, turbulence cannot be forecast. For this reason, I also suggest that if you walk around the cabin, you steady yourself with one hand by keeping it on the seat backs you pass.

You may experience several kinds of fear during cruise. People who are afraid of heights and reject the idea that the air has mass and that the plane is kept in the air because of the lift provided by the wings may sit anxiously and rigidly waiting for the plane to confirm their beliefs by falling out of the sky. Even the slightest bit of turbulence confirms the faulty hypothesis, and they react with panicky thoughts and an out-of-control body. If this is your problem, snap those thoughts away with your rubber band, control your breathing, and get back in touch with the rational side of your brain. You may want to use a mantra such as, "I'm safe; the plane cannot fall. I'm safe; the plane cannot fall. I'm safe; the plane cannot fall," and so on.

The person who is claustrophobic or who has panic attacks may become panicky because the pilot, while telling passengers the altitude of the plane, may also mention how many hours and minutes it will be before landing. This is when the thoughts about being trapped, not having enough air, and having a heart attack and dying may come up. Concentrate on your breathing for several minutes and then reconsider your irrational thoughts. The absolute worst thing that can happen is that you will hyperventilate and pass out. While this may be embarrassing, at least you will spend a portion of the trip in relative comfort…at least until you regain consciousness (this is a joke!).

The cruise is the best time to work on your fears. Once you get yourself under control, determine your SUDS score, and then, using various techniques (the RED technique, the Valsalva maneuver, thought stopping, and muscle relaxation) try to lower your SUDS score by 1 point. If it is at 8, try to lower it to 7. When you get to 7, try to lower it to 6, and so on. If you learn that you are in control of your thoughts and your physical reactions, you have taken a huge step toward eliminating your fear. If you feel like your fear is under control, systematically look at all the things you are afraid of as you cruise: invite your fear to fly with you.

Under no circumstances should you suppress your fear during this phase of your recovery. Don't play loud music, talk incessantly to the person sitting next to you, or distract yourself with crossword puzzles. Attend to your fearful thoughts and the physical reactions to them. Learn that you can control them.

If your fearful thoughts do not subside with the strategies outlined earlier (RED technique, Valsalva maneuver, and the like), you may want to try a strategy discussed in chapter 8: worry time. This begins by identifying the intrusive thoughts that are scaring you, noting the time on your watch (yes, you'll need it now), and then concentrating on subvocally repeating the worrisome thought as often as you can in five minutes. While this seems like a risky approach on the surface, most fearful fliers cannot engage in this technique for five minutes without realizing how silly the thoughts are and discontinuing their worrying. However, if this strategy increases your panicky thoughts, discontinue the practice and return to controlling your breathing.

If you find that you are relaxing a bit but cannot get comfortable, is it because you are still "flying the plane" by looking out the window, listening to every noise, and monitoring the flight attendants' faces, looking for signs of panic? You may want to use a version of worry time. Repeat over and over, "I must monitor every phase of this flight or the plane will crash." As you do this, switch systematically from monitoring the wings to see if they are still attached to listening to the engines to make sure that they are still running to watching the flight attendants' faces to make sure they are still calm. Do this until you are absolutely sick of it.

Turbulence

Pilots measure turbulence on a 0–6 scale, and on every flight plan, there is a *turbulence index* (TI), which is an estimate of the turbulence along the route of flight. This index is determined partially by looking at weather and partially as a result of reports from pilots who, earlier in the day, flew the route you are taking. A TI of 0 indicates that either no or very light turbulence is expected, and a 6 indicates very heavy turbulence. Planes are not dispatched into areas where heavy turbulence (T6) is expected, and so far as it is possible, moderate turbulence is avoided by taking alternate routes. Why is it avoided? Is turbulence dangerous? No, it isn't! Dispatchers and pilots want you to have the most comfortable ride possible and will take alternate routes that may cause schedule delays to make sure this happens.

How can you measure turbulence yourself? Order a glass of water that is filled almost full. If the TI is T0 or T1, the water will barely move. As the TI approaches T2, the water will begin to move, and as it approaches T4, it will spill, sometimes in substantial quantities. When the flight attendants pick up cups and dishes because of turbulence, they are expecting something greater than a 1 or 2 and are doing this so that things won't spill on you, not because the plane will fall out of the sky. Also, when the captain asks the flight attendants to take their seats, he is ensuring that they will not be injured, not making the request because the plane is in danger.

What should you do during turbulence? Do not use your rubber band to stop your thoughts; the palm of your hand will become quite sore very quickly. Also, do not go into the brace position by becoming very rigid, hanging on to the armrests for dear life, and placing your foot against the seat support in front of you. Do fasten your seat belt very tightly because this will increase your feeling of security. Additionally you may assume the "Jell-O" position in order to move with the turbulence.

The Jell-O position involves relaxing any muscles that are particularly tense, putting your hands loosely at your side or on the armrests, and pretending that you are a Jell-O mold quivering with the rhythm of the turbulence. In other words, try to be totally relaxed and move with the plane.

Moving in response to the plane can be done either with music or without it. My wife, Sandra, plays an ancient tape of Jerry Lee Lewis', "Whole Lotta Shakin' Goin' On," and moves in rhythm with the music to remind her that, while the plane may shake in turbulence, it is not a dangerous phenomenon (just a whole lot of shaking). You may wish to choose some other music or simply move with the rhythm of the turbulence when it occurs. Will you look stupid if you "dance" with the rhythm of turbulence? How can it be stupid to deal with your fear?

Finally, an extremely effective way to deal with the fear that builds during turbulence is to develop a mantra that reminds you that turbulence is not a safety issue. Two that I recommend are, "It's a comfort issue" or "It's a service issue." By repeating these sayings, you are reminded that turbulence is not a safety issue even though it is not comfortable, or that, while turbulence may disrupt the service and you may not get your meal or your drink, it will not knock the plane from the sky.

Descent

The descent is the favorite part of the flight for most people, including fearful fliers. Perhaps the first thing that will cue you that the descent has begun is that the engine noise is reduced. In fact, the engines are pulled back to idle for much of the descent, and the plane is actually gliding. The captain never shuts the engines off. If you are extremely sensitive to the movement of the plane, you may also notice that the captain has lowered the nose of the aircraft. One sure cue that the descent has begun is that you begin to develop a stuffy feeling in your ear. As the cabin pressure is lowered, a disequilibrium among the pressure in your outer, middle, and inner ears develops. Swallowing hard or yawning will equalize this pressure in most instances as will pinching your nose and blowing as though you are blowing into a handkerchief. Begin by blowing gently, gradually increasing the pressure until you can hear properly.

One thing that you may experience during the descent to the runway is an *expedited descent*. This occurs when ATC wants the plane at an altitude that cannot be attained using typical descent procedures. What happens is that the captain deploys the *spoilers* or *speed brakes*, which are rectangular metal structures on the wing, and they pop up into the air passing over the wing. This "spoils" the lift, and the plane descends more rapidly. Again, what you need to do if you suspect that spoilers have been deployed is to look out the window. Do not look out the window if you are afraid of heights, but others may wish to verify that the spoilers are deployed (they will be near the leading edge of the wing and about one third of the way down the wing). They are several feet long and, as noted before, are rectangular.

One unexpected event during descent is that your plane might be put into a holding pattern. As noted earlier, most delays are on-ground delays that occur prior to takeoff. But occasionally you will be nearing your destination, and ATC will determine that it is not safe to have all inbound traffic continue toward the airport and will ask the captain to enter a holding pattern, which is nothing more than flying in circles or flying *vectors* (a zigzag pattern rather than a straight line). In addition to the idea of being in the sky longer, which can produce fearful thoughts, you may become alarmed if you look out the window and see other planes that seem to be quite near flying the same pattern as your plane. In the circular holding pattern, planes are stacked at 1,000-foot intervals and are in no danger of colliding. If your thoughts get panicky, snap your rubber band, control your breathing, and remind yourself that all the planes in the stack are being observed via ATC radar and that your plane is equipped with TCAS to avoid the possibility of midair collisions. Incidentally, the plane at the lowest altitude will land first, and then the other planes will descend 1,000 feet to the next circle and so on until all the planes are safely down.

During descent there are likely to be several intermediate level-offs just as there were during the climb. When this happens, the nose of the plane will come up and the engines will be returned to cruise power. Many people mistakenly believe that the plane is starting to climb again when this occurs, but this is not the case. At 10,000 feet, you will hear a single chime. This will be repeated at 1,500 feet. You will also hear the flaps deployed several (perhaps as many as five) times during the descent.

There are several things that occur during the final phase of the flight that may scare you. One of these is that the plane *wallows*, or rocks back and forth. This does not mean that the plane is out of control. The control surfaces of the wing are more sensitive at slower speeds and reduced power, and this produces this movement. Also, the captain is making minor corrections to ensure that the plane will land in exactly the right location on the runway.

If you are looking out the window from the rear, you may observe that the plane appears to be flying "at an angle" instead of straight toward the runway. Whenever the plane is landing and there is a cross-wind, the captain puts the plane into a *crab*. The plane is flying toward the center of the runway, but the nose of the plane is not pointed directly at the runway. The crab is removed just before touchdown, the wing pointing toward the crosswind is lowered, and the plane touches down on one wheel quickly followed by the other. This is the classic crosswind landing, which is performed safely hundreds of times each day.

Perhaps the scariest thing that can occur during descent is when the landing is rejected and the pilot performs what is known as a *go around*. This typically occurs because there is another plane on the runway, and it is illegal for the captain to land with another plane on the runway. The maneuver is a simple one and occurs every day. The pilot simply pushes the throttle forward to full power, pulls back on the yoke, enters a pre-determined airspace, and returns to the landing queue. Go arounds can also occur because weather conditions change (e.g., crosswinds pick up, to the point of being unsafe, or the pilot does not feel that he or she can land safely for other reasons). One pilot rejected a landing at Raleigh-Durham International Airport because a deer was on the runway.

When a landing is rejected, you are typically on final approach and the landing gear has been lowered. Suddenly, the power comes up, the landing gear is retracted, and the plane begins to climb. What you should know is that for every landing, there is a plan for a rejected landing, and at every airport, certain airspace is reserved for rejected landings. So even though a rejected landing is startling and may be scary, it is perfectly safe.

If a normal landing is to occur, the landing gear is lowered with a thump, bump, thump a few hundred feet above the ground, the nose of the aircraft is lifted, and the power increased. As you may know if you have observed aircrafts landing, modern jetliners and commuters land first on their rear wheels after which the nose is lowered until the small wheel on the front touches the runway.

Taxi In

At touchdown, the *reversers* are deployed to reverse the thrust of the engines, which provides braking action. Also, the speed brakes (or spoilers) on the wings come up automatically to reduce the lift the wing is providing with the result that the weight of the airplane is on the wheels. Then, as the plane slows, the brakes are used to slow it further. The brakes are extremely powerful, and you will move forward in your seat when they are applied. You will also hear them screech and grind as they take hold. Within a few seconds, the captain will turn the plane off the runway, retract the flaps, which were fully extended at landing, and taxi to the gate. You will be advised by an announcement from the flight deck to stay in your seats until the plane is safely parked at the gate (please follow this advice no matter how badly you want to get out). Finally, the seat-belt sign will go off, the door will open, and you will deplane.

All you need do at this point in the flight is to congratulate yourself on flying. If you are a perfectionist, you may begin to criticize yourself for not functioning as well as you "should have" on the plane. Use your rubber band to snap away these irrational thoughts, and then congratulate yourself on your accomplishment.

CHAPTER 10

Developing Your Flight Plan and Using Guided Imagery

Preparation and information are the keys to having a successful flight. In chapters 5–7, I gave you the best available information about airplanes, personnel, and the industry. The bottom line is that, while flying is not perfect, it is safer than alternative modes of transportation. For example, in 2007 (the latest date for which statistics are available at this writing) there were more than 11.2 million flights and no fatalities (National Transportation Safety Board 2008); 30,401 deaths in automobiles or 1.37 deaths per million miles traveled (FARS 2008); and 708 deaths in rail accidents or 3.05 deaths per million miles traveled (Federal Railroad Administration Office of Safety Analysis 2008). You have also been given specific techniques for coping with your physical and mental reactions to your fear. Hopefully, if you have anticipatory anxiety, you have started working on that problem using the strategies outlined in chapter 8. Now it is time to prepare for your graduation from fearful flier to confident flier. In chapter 9, I took you through a dress rehearsal of your first successful flight. Now, I want you to engage in the final stages of preparation for the flight.

CHOOSING SUPPORT PERSONS

A major question for many people is, "Should I fly with another person?" Generally, yes, but there are some factors to consider here. One of these is whether you have a person who can fly with you who will be 100 percent supportive of you, regardless of your behavior. The last thing you need to be worrying about is whether your behavior will be approved of by the people around you, particularly the person who is supposed to be supportive. A support person, if properly briefed, can help you use your flight plan and make the entire experience more bearable. Support people can also be rich sources of pleasant memories as you reflect on your victory.

Generally, I suggest that you not fly with your spouse, parents, or children. If you get frightened before the flight, people who love you are likely to give you permission to avoid the flight because they see the pain you are in. Unfortunately, having someone say, "You don't have to do this today" may be all the reason you need to avoid the flight. Lifelong friends and nonjudgmental relatives provide the best support.

SETTING GOALS

As strange as it may seem, setting goals for the flight on which you will confront your fear will probably be difficult. Before I go into this topic in detail, I want you to take a few minutes and think about your last flight, if you have ever taken one. Consider each phase of the flight, taxi, takeoff, cruise, and landing. How frightened were you at each of these stages? Using your SUDS score (1 is completely relaxed, and 10 is totally scared), rate your fear at each of these stages. Also, write out other problems you experienced, such as sweaty palms, tense muscles, and light-headedness during the flight.

Stages of the Flight	SUDS Score
Taxiing	_____
Taking off	_____
Cruising	_____
Landing	_____
Other problems	

_____

_____

_____

After you have thought about how scared you were and how you reacted to your fear, begin to consider your goals for your graduation flight. Do not expect to function perfectly on this flight. I have seen people who had made tremendous advances against their fear declare privately, and then publicly, that they had failed. But is it "failure" to get on a plane for the first time in years, to fly alcohol and drug free for the first time, to grab the seat once as the plane encountered some bumpy air (when previously that person had hung on for dear life throughout the flight)? Yes, some people count themselves as failures when they do not fly "perfectly." Do not allow yourself to fall into this terrible trap. Reward yourself for small victories.

Consider now the goals for your graduation flight. Perhaps, instead of holding onto the seat in sheer terror, your goal should be to deal with the fear you experience on takeoff and reduce your SUDS score from 10 to 7. Perhaps your goal should be to rock and roll with the turbulence and remind yourself that turbulence is not a safety issue. Perhaps it should be to close the shade and remind yourself that planes cannot fall. You may even want to check the wings once in a while, because, if you recall our lesson on aerodynamics, planes cannot fall like a brick if the wings are attached. What follows are some sample goals:

1. Reduce my SUDS score by 3 points during the takeoff roll and actual takeoff by controlling my physical responses to the fear.

2. Move with the turbulence and remind myself, "It's a comfort issue, not a safety issue."

3. Take a flight sober, and control my responses rather than letting them control me.

4. Take a flight without checking the weather channel for thunderstorms.

5. Get on a plane and fly, and work on my responses using my flight plan.

Take some time at this point to set a goal or goals for your next flight.

My Goal(s) for My Flight from Fear

_____

_____

_____

_____

_____

_____

CHOOSING YOUR WEAPONS AGAINST FEAR

In chapter 4, I outlined several techniques to control various reactions to your fear, including controlled breathing, thought-stopping strategies, relaxing tense muscles, and using the Valsalva maneuver to slow a racing heart. You will need some or all of these techniques in your flight plan. What follows are my recommendations for the approach you should use on the plane. As you will see, these vary to some degree by problem type.

Strategies: Crashing and Dying and Acrophobia

Recurring and sometimes racing thoughts that something absolutely catastrophic is about to happen to the plane (which will kill you and everyone on board) drive this fear. Your first line of defense should probably be thought stopping. Thought stopping should be followed by controlling your breathing to calm yourself, and then muscle relaxation to relieve the tension that has developed in the muscles. If concerns about turbulence are a part of your fear, you also need to include in your flight plan the idea of moving or dancing when turbulence occurs.

Do not use thought stopping as a means to control your response to turbulence except as a last resort, because you need to snap your rubber band with vigor (it has to hurt) if it is to be effective, and you can pulverize your palm if the turbulence lasts several minutes.

You may also want to consider other things to do prior to and during the flight. I've already mentioned meeting the pilot. Many fearful fliers feel better if they can look into the eyes of the pilot. It is probably better not to tell them that you are afraid because some "smart-alecky" pilot may respond by telling you that he or she is also afraid. Please do not insult the crew, as one fearful flier did, by asking them if they have been drinking. It is certainly okay to ask questions about turbulence and weather en route as well as whether they expect the flight to be on time.

You should also meet the flight attendant in the area where you are sitting and perhaps confide that you are a nervous flier. This provides you with a link to the crew, which some people find reassuring.

Sample Flight Plan: Fear of the Plane Falling or Crashing

When I Board the Plane

1. Greet the pilot.

2. Meet the flight attendant.

3. Close the blind covering the window (not permitted until after takeoff).

If the Fear Comes

1. Use thought stopping:

   a. Snap rubber band.

   b. Subvocally yell "Stop!"

   c. Use a positive self-statement: "I can do this!"

2. Control breathing (five to seven minutes).

3. Relax breathing muscles if light-headedness persists.

If Turbulence Comes

1. Move; don't hang on to arms of seat.

2. Repeat this mantra: "This is not a safety issue. It only makes me uncomfortable."

3. Check the wings. If they are still attached, say, "I'm okay."

Strategies: Claustrophobia

As you know, this fear is driven by recurring thoughts that you will run out of air and suffocate. This is the tightness in the throat and chest you feel when your breathing becomes quick and shallow; it causes your racing thoughts to increase. Your flight plan should begin with controlling your breathing. If you still feel a bit light-headed after five minutes, you will want to focus on relaxing the muscles in the throat, chest, and abdomen that are involved in the breathing process. Thought stopping should only be used if you feel like you are losing control of your body. I also recommend that you ask the flight attendant to bring you a glass of ice after you are seated. Ice on the tongue can make you feel much cooler.

You also need to consider boarding the plane just before takeoff (remember to check in so they do not give your seat to someone else). Try never to enter the jet bridge when it is crowded, particularly on a warm day, and, once you are in your seat, turn on the small eyeball vent above your head and direct the flow of air onto your face. Remember that when you begin to feel warm, your fear may be heightened.

Sample Flight Plan: Claustrophobia

When I Board the Plane

1. Board last.

2. Do not enter a crowded jet bridge.

3. Turn the air onto my face.

If the Fear Comes

1. Control my breathing (five to seven minutes).

2. If light-headedness persists, relax breathing muscles.

If Panic Comes

1. Use thought stopping:

   a. Snap rubber band.

   b. Subvocally yell "Stop!"

   c. Use a positive self-statement: Yes, "I can control my breathing!"

2. Return to controlling my breathing.

Strategies: Fear of Panic Attacks

This fear is driven by thoughts such as, "I will have a panic attack and die," "I will embarrass myself," or "I will lose my mind and end up in a comatose state." It is sometimes accompanied by concerns about having a heart attack. Your flight plan should begin by relaxing tense muscles (throat, chest, and abdomen) that can alter the breathing process, followed by controlling your breathing. You may also include the Valsalva maneuver if you are afraid that you will have a heart attack and have consulted with your physician about your cardiovascular health. Remember, the Valsalva maneuver must be followed by controlling your breathing for five to seven minutes if it is to be effective.

Sample Flight Plan: Panic Attacks

When I Board the Plane

1. Remind myself, "I'm in control."

2. Turn the air onto my face.

3. Relax tense muscles.

If the Fear Comes

1. Control breathing (five to seven minutes).

2. If light-headedness persists, relax muscles that control breathing process.

If Panic Comes

1. Use thought stopping:

   a. Snap rubber band.

   b. Subvocally yell "Stop!"

   c. Use positive self-statement: "I'm in control of my body."

The three flight plans shown in this section are only samples. By now you should understand your thoughts and physical responses to them. When you board the flight, you should have your own flight plan that is geared to your particular concerns. Why should you do this? You may recall the discussion of what happens to your brain when you become afraid: You cannot access stored information. Leave nothing to chance. Develop your own flight plan.

BEFORE THE FLIGHT: USING GUIDED IMAGERY

In a very real sense, the conquest of your fear begins with your imagination. The cliché "If you can imagine it, you can do it" is accurate. If you can imagine yourself being victorious over your fear, you can do it.

The fear of flying is unlike any other fear in one regard: you cannot take only part of a flight. The KLM (Royal Dutch Airlines) program uses flight simulators, which is an excellent approach to approximating flight. Imaginary flights taken while sitting in a comfortable chair can also be very helpful. These, if done properly, will evoke all the mental and physical responses that occur on a real flight and allow you to practice dealing with them in a nonthreatening environment. But ultimately you must take off and fly.

If you have anticipatory anxiety and have made a reservation to fly, you probably are already taking imaginary flights, but in most (maybe all) instances, these imaginary flights are failures because they end in disaster. Disastrous imaginary flights only reinforce the fear and add to your suffering. These flights must be replaced with successful imaginary flights.

Before you take your first imaginary flight, take at least one practice trip to the airport so that the sights and sounds of the trip and the airport are familiar to you. Also, make your reservation so that you know your destination. It will also help to know the type of plane you will be flying so you can visualize both its exterior and interior.

Write out your self-guided imagery. Before you actually embark on your imaginary flight, make an outline of what you want to imagine, such as the one that follows:

1. Leaving the house (allowing plenty of time to get to the airport)

2. Taking the trip to the airport (with landmarks that I will see)

3. Parking (with alternatives in mind if lot is full)

4. Entering the airport (noticing sights and sounds)

5. Passing through security (noticing sights and sounds)

6. Waiting at the gate area (noticing sights and sounds and using my flight plan)

7. Boarding (noticing sights and sounds and using my flight plan)

8. Pushing back and taxiing (noticing sights, smells, and sounds and using my flight plan)

9. Taking off (noticing sensations and sounds and using my flight plan)

10. Cruising (noticing sights, sensations, and sounds and using my flight plan)

11. Experiencing turbulence (noticing sensations and using my flight plan)

12. Descending and landing (noticing sights, sounds, and sensations and using my flight plan)

The idea is to imagine each aspect of the flight, your reaction to it, and your coping response to the fear that may arise as your flight progresses. The following self-guided imagery can serve as a model for your own imagery:

My luggage is in the car. I make a last-minute check of my apartment, lock the door, and get into my car. I start the car, back out of my parking spot, and pull onto the street. I pass the ugly purple chicken sign, then enter the freeway at the 14th Street on-ramp, and the traffic is light, as it always is early in the morning. As I drive to the airport, I see a plane rise into the sky and my fear rises. I snap my rubber band and yell, "Stop!" I can handle air travel.

Twenty minutes after I leave home, I pull into the long-term parking lot, park my car, and, with my carry-on luggage, catch the shuttle to the terminal. I leave the shuttle, enter the airport, move through security (where I hear the shrill sound of the metal detectors' alarms that keep going off), and move quickly to the gate area. Several people have already arrived at the gate area, and, because I am a bit early, I continue to walk down the concourse to ease the tension that is beginning to build. As I return, I hear the announcement, "Ladies and gentlemen, we will be boarding our Chicago flight by row numbers today." I give my boarding pass to the gate agent, but I wait to board the plane until the final call for passenger boarding.

After the announcement, "Ladies and gentlemen, all passengers holding tickets on this flight should be on board at this time," I enter the jet bridge, which is quite warm. I move quickly to the plane, step on, turn, pass through the first-class cabin, find my seat, and stow my carry-on luggage in the overhead compartment. I take my seat, fasten the seat belt, and turn the vent that is over my head on so that the air goes onto my face.

I hear the announcement, "Flight attendants, please prepare for departure." Because my anxiety is rising, I use my skills to work on calming my breathing. I begin to feel the tension subside and I remind myself there is plenty of air in the cabin. The flight attendants make the safety announcements, and I look around and locate the emergency exits.

The announcement, "Flight attendants, prepare for takeoff," and a single chime indicates we are ready for the takeoff roll. The engine noise comes up, and we start to roll. Immediately, I hear "Bump, bump, bump" as the landing gear rolls over the lights in the middle of the runway.

The pilot pulls back on the yoke, the nose comes up, and we are flying. There is a thud as the landing gear extends to the end of the struts and then other thuds as it is raised and locked into place. The high-pitched sounds of the hydraulic pumps remind me that devices on the wings are being retracted.

Seconds later, the pilot lowers the nose of the plane and pulls back on the power. There is that hated feeling in the pit of my stomach. I concentrate on slowing my breathing and remind myself that we are still climbing. I hear a single chime as we pass through 1,500 feet and another as we pass through 10,000 feet. The plane bumps a bit as we encounter some choppy air. I remind myself that turbulence is only a comfort issue, not a safety issue.

I hear a single chime, and the pilot announces that a smooth flight is expected but asks, "Please keep your seat belt fastened when in your seat." People get out of their seats, and the flight attendants start to serve beverages and snacks. The plane bumps a bit as we encounter some rough air, and the seat-belt sign comes on. I remind myself to tighten my seat-belt. Suddenly the bumps are closer together. I turn on my CD player and start to move with the turbulence. I repeat, "It's a comfort issue. It's a comfort issue. It's a comfort issue," over and over again, as the plane cruises toward my destination.

The noise outside the plane has lessened, and we are definitely descending. The pressure in my ears builds, and I swallow hard to relieve it. The captain thanks us for flying his airline and reminds us that the seat-belt sign is on and our seat belts should be fastened. I swallow again to relieve the pressure. I hear the hydraulic pumps again, and then again. We are definitely approaching the airport. I work on controlling my breathing because I feel the fear rising.

The whine of the hydraulic pumps of my B-737 and the thump-bump-thump of the landing gear coming down signals that we are about to land. I'm excited! I've done it and better than I expected. I can fly!!!! We touch down with a thump, engine noise comes up, brakes squeak and grind, and we turn off the runway. We taxi quickly to the gate. I hear the announcement, "Please stay in your seats until we are parked safely at the gate," followed by, "Flight attendants, please prepare for arrival." The plane stops, the doors open, and I deplane. It feels so-o-o-o good.

Your imagery should be written with your own problems in mind and may vary significantly from the imagined flight you just read. Two things are important. First, take a complete flight and imagine those parts of the flight that will be difficult for you. Second, actually use the skills in your flight plan to cope with the imagined reactions that you have. This means that you should review your flight plan before each imagined scene, place a rubber band over your palm, and be prepared to slow your racing heart or to relax your tense muscles. At this time, write out the self-guided imagery that you will use to practice for your graduation flight.

My Successful Flight Imagery

_____

_____

_____

_____

_____

_____

_____

_____

_____

_____

_____

_____

_____

_____

_____

_____

_____

_____

_____

_____

_____

_____

After you have written your imagery, you may wish to record and then play it as you practice. The recording can be used to cue the visual images that you experience. The practice sessions can occur anywhere as long as you will be undisturbed during them. Prior to the imagery, you should take several deep breaths and then let the air out of your lungs as slowly as possible. If you have muscle tension, tense and relax the areas where the tension exists to make yourself as comfortable as possible. Once you are relaxed, "run the visual tape" of your imagery. After each session, assess how you did using your SUDS (1–10) scale.

If you find that you are not coping satisfactorily with your imaginary flight, review the skills discussed in chapter 4 to make sure you are using them properly. If you are, keep practicing. You may also wish to review your information base. Sometimes one nagging thought (for example, "The air traffic control system is unsafe") can keep you from moving forward. If you have doubts, find a pilot, air traffic controller, or other expert to chat with about your concerns.

There is no formula for how many imaginary flights you will need to complete. I suggest that you practice once per day for at least two weeks prior to your flight. However, remember that self-guided imagery should be included among the strategies you use to combat your fear.

CHAPTER 11

After Your First Successful Flight

After you complete your first successful flight, by which I mean a flight that corresponds to your objectives, the fight has just begun. I've already suggested that once you start flying, you need to continue flying regularly. One fearful flier took this advice so seriously that the week after his first successful flight, he flew from Boston to Dallas, Dallas to Miami, Miami to San Juan and back, and then from Miami to Boston. Was this necessary? No, but he had regained his ability to fly once before and then lost it because he did not fly enough. He vowed he would never allow that to happen to him again. In this chapter, I will talk more about how often and how far you should be flying to help you maintain your gains and continue to advance in your battle with your fear. However, continuing to fly is only one of an extensive list of things you need to do to make sure that you accomplish your goal of flying without fear. Each of the areas you need to tackle as you continue your recovery will be addressed.

HOW MUCH SHOULD YOU FLY?

Based on experience with and feedback from people who took successful graduation flights in our fearful flier seminars, we developed a recommendation: fly within three months of your first successful flight. This recommendation was specifically for those people who boarded the graduation flight and met or exceeded their own expectations (goals) and for those people who could state with a high level of confidence that when they next flew, they were sure that they could board their planes and handle whatever came. If you have flown and met your own goals, the "fly within three months" recommendation still holds.

If you have completed a successful flight, are not 100 percent certain that you can board a plane in the future, but feel that you probably can, the recommendation is that you fly immediately, perhaps within a week of your first flight. This is because confidence can erode with the passage of time.

If you fly within three months and things go well—what then? To maintain your confidence after your first two flights, fly at least once or twice a year, even if the flight is only for the purpose of keeping your fear grounded. However, if you are not doing well after your first two flights, it may be time to seek some professional help unless you can identify the irrational thoughts that make you uncomfortable when you fly. If you can determine the problem, continue to work on it by getting accurate information and, of course, by continuing to fly.

Some of the problems that contribute to the fear of flying are more resistant than others. Turbulence leads the list of resistant problems, so do not be surprised or discouraged if your fear of turbulence persists for a bit longer than your other concerns. Many fearful fliers take several flights spaced over several months to get over their concerns about turbulence. If turbulence continues to be a concern after three or four flights, review the causes of turbulence and begin to try to predict its occurrence. For example, when you fly over a mountain range, you are almost certain to hit some bumpy air. Try to predict when this will occur rather than sitting in your seat in dread of turbulence. You can also predict mild turbulence whenever the temperature on the ground is very warm (think Phoenix in the summer). Also, if there are small, innocuous-looking, white, powder-puff clouds in the sky, you are likely to encounter modest turbulence when your plane takes off or lands. It may also help you to ask the pilot if turbulence is expected during the next portion of the flight. As mentioned earlier, each flight plan has turbulence indexes for each segment of the flight, so the pilot has some indication of what to expect. If you are told that some turbulence is expected when the plane takes off and that it will continue during the flight, combat any fear that arises with the mantra, "Turbulence is a comfort issue." Importantly, keep moving with the turbulence. It is only a "Whole Lotta Shakin' Goin' On!"

WORKING ON CONTRIBUTORY FEARS

In chapters 1 and 2, I noted that aerophobia is only one of the contributors to the fear of flying. This section revisits and extends that earlier discussion by once again emphasizing the complexity of the issue for some people.

Specific Phobias

Not all fearful fliers have a phobic reaction to flying but, for those who do, the reaction may stem from a variety of issues. In some instances, people who are claustrophobic or acrophobic are also afraid that the airplane will crash (aerophobia), so they have multiple concerns. If you are not flying because of the contributory fears of being in enclosed spaces and at a height, or if you have one of these fears and are also afraid the airplane will crash, this is a good time to begin an ambitious, vigorous attack on these concerns because by doing so, you can totally or partially alleviate your fear of flying. Fortunately, these phobias are relatively easy to treat.

There are at least three approaches that have been used by therapists to treat specific phobias, including both claustrophobia and acrophobia. These are *in vivo desensitization* (a gradual exposure to the stimulus that arouses the fear), *counter conditioning* (exposing a person to the feared stimulus via imagery while they are in a relaxed state), and *emotional flooding* (inducing and maintaining the fear under the supervision of the therapist). Of these three procedures, I prefer in vivo desensitization, which involves actually exposing yourself to the feared situation but in a controlled fashion.

Recently I helped a woman who was afraid of elevators and airplanes work on her fear of elevators and other enclosed spaces. I began this process by having her develop an *exposure hierarchy*, which is a ranking of fearful situations from those that are least scary to those that produce the greatest amount of fear. What follows is the hierarchy she constructed:

1. Glass elevator in shopping mall that only goes up and down one story

2. New elevators that go up no more than five stories

3. New elevators that go up or down more than five stories

4. New elevators without telephones

5. Old elevators that go up only one or two stories

6. Old elevators that "drop" before they go up (meaning that, as the control mechanism on the elevator releases prior to ascending, the elevator seems to sink or start down)

7. Old elevators that go up more than two stories and do not have telephones

After she developed the hierarchy, we worked out a plan for her to "expose" herself to a series of elevators. However, prior to the time when she began to ride elevators, we reviewed the relaxation techniques she had learned to address her fear of flying (which are the techniques discussed in chapter 4). It was essential that when she was riding elevators or entering other enclosed spaces, she felt that she could control her mental and physical reactions to her fear if the unthinkable happened and the elevator became stuck. Most importantly, she needed to control her breathing during elevator "rides" to keep herself calm.

By now I'm sure that you know that I do not want you to expose yourself to a fearful situation if you do not have a plan to cope with the fear. After our review, my client was asked to ride elevators, beginning with the one-story glass elevator in the shopping mall. After she had mastered the shopping mall elevator, I urged her to take the next step, which was to ride a new elevator up five stories, get off, reboard the elevator, and ride it to the ground floor. This process was repeated until she felt a sense of mastery over new elevators. She was then asked to take subsequent steps when she felt ready to do so. If at any point in the process she felt that she was unable to handle a problem that developed, I accompanied her on the elevator until she developed the confidence that she needed to complete the task on her own. If at any time during the process she experienced a setback, which was defined as either avoiding an elevator that she felt she had mastered or feeling extremely panicky

(8–10 SUDS score) on an elevator that she felt she had mastered, she went back to a less frightening step on the hierarchy and built up her confidence level again.

In a totally self-administered treatment, another woman eliminated her claustrophobia by following a program that I outlined. At the outset, not only would this woman not ride an elevator, she avoided all situations in which she was cramped or confined or thought she might become so. She now takes all types of elevators, including those in the tallest buildings in New York City.

The exposure approach also works with acrophobia. I know because I used it to help myself deal with my own fear of heights. I first became aware that I was acrophobic when I attended a college basketball game and was seated in a very steep upper balcony overlooking the floor. I spent the entire night with my arm hooked over the back of my seat so I would not "fall," which was physically impossible. I also had a bit of a shock some years later when I boarded the glass elevator that runs up the outside of the Fairmont Hotel in San Francisco. Because the hotel sits on one of the largest hills in San Francisco, the elevator is quickly very high above the city as it starts toward the top of the hotel. I looked down once, pressed myself against the back wall of the elevator, and hoped the ride would end quickly. I overcame this fear by gradually exposing myself to higher and higher places, both in glass elevators and in open spaces, being careful not to go too far beyond my comfort level. I am still not totally comfortable looking down from a height of ten stories when I am in an open area such as the top of a building. However, I will lean over the balcony and look down to the floor or sidewalk below in spite of my fear. Best of all, I love glass elevators and would recommend them to anyone who is not afraid of heights.

If you have a specific phobia, develop your own exposure hierarchy in the spaces provided:

1. _____

2. _____

3. _____

4. _____

5. _____

6. _____

7. _____

8. _____

9. _____

10. _____

Next develop a timetable for confronting your fear. Move ahead as quickly as you can but never move so fast that you "overrun" your confidence. The best way to determine whether you are ready to proceed is to use the 1–10 SUDS scale introduced in chapter 4. Ask yourself this question, "On a 1–10 scale, with 1 being no confidence and 10 being complete confidence, how confident am I that I can handle the next step on my exposure hierarchy?" If your confidence rating is less than 7, I suggest that you spend more time working on the current step. It is important that you also allow yourself the opportunity to be spontaneous. If, for example, an opportunity presents itself to take the next step a bit earlier than you had planned, but you are 100 percent confident that you can be successful, do it. Admittedly, this is a bit of a risk, but what you are trying to accomplish is to begin to trust yourself. It's no fun to allow your fear to control you.

Sometimes you may reach a point in your exposure hierarchy where you seem to be stuck, that is, you cannot move to the next, more difficult step. If this happens, you may need to insert a "bridge." Your bridge may be taking the next step with a support person or hiring a therapist to help you get unstuck. Usually, however, it only means spending more time on the current step and practicing your relaxation skills. Controlling your physiological response to fear may give you the confidence you need to move ahead. The statement, "I'm scared, but I'm doing it," is often heard from people who are facing their fear. Some are ashamed that they have a fear of their fear and are therefore embarrassed to admit that they are still afraid. However, the person who moves ahead in the face of fear is truly courageous and should be patting him- or herself on the back.

Another approach that helps some people who are having trouble moving up their exposure hierarchy is to spend so much time at the point where they are stuck that they become bored. Boredom with the current step plus the desire to take the next step in the process of conquering fear may provide the motivation needed to help you move on if you get stuck.

Finally, never push yourself so hard that you avoid the task that you have set for yourself. As I have pointed out, avoidance is the primary mechanism involved in heightening your fear because of the physical relief that occurs after you avoid. If you do avoid a task, lower your sights by going back to a step on your hierarchy that you are confident you can perform and rebuild your confidence.

Panic Attacks

If you are having panic attacks and have not consulted a good cognitive behavioral therapist, I suggest that you do so immediately, even if you are on medication that is helping. As you know by now, my philosophy is to use medication as an adjunct, not as the sole approach, to therapy. A skilled cognitive behavioral therapy (CBT) therapist helped one of my daughters eliminate her panic attacks within a few months, without medication. She chose this approach not out of opposition to medication, but because of her hypersensitivity to any type of medication and fear of side effects. Not surprisingly, she learned during the course of her therapy that her irrational, perfectionistic beliefs were at the core of her problem. Once she learned that being perfect is impossible for mortals, she began to turn the situation around. She has been free of panic attacks for many years, primarily because she learned to deal with her irrational thinking and learned that she could control her body.

TRUST AND CONTROL

People who are afraid to fly often have control issues that, when examined carefully, are related to their inability to trust people. A *control issue* is defined in this context as a continuing effort to control both the human and physical aspects of one's environment. For example, people with a control issue often insist on driving when they go places with friends or family members. There are two ways to deal with this problem. One of these is getting information from a credible source to vigorously counter the faulty logic. If you believe that you are safer in your own car because you have control of the steering wheel, it is time to really take a look at the illusion you have created for yourself and to begin to dispute your beliefs. There is no comparison between the degree of control you have in your car to the controls placed on the pilot of your plane.

If getting information to counter your fears is not sufficient, I recommend that you take up the matter with a therapist. The objective of this therapy should be to confront the logic that limits your ability to trust others. My experience suggests that people who have difficulty trusting others have either been traumatized by caregivers (e.g., physical abuse) or have experienced extreme and painful hurt in their relationships with others (e.g., left by wife). The end result of the therapy should be that you develop a new approach to evaluating the world in general and to your relationships with significant people in your life.

YOU AND THE MEDIA

There will be airline disasters in the future. There will also be stories about the industry that are unfavorable. Because I want you to be an informed flier who votes for safety with your purchase of a ticket, I urge you to get as much information as you can about the industry and to lobby your local and national representatives to work to improve airline safety. However, I recommend against watching or reading detailed reports of disasters, particularly those that are printed or shown on television a day or two after a disaster.

The foregoing sentence has been my standard recommendation for years. However, on January 15, 2009, my opinion changed a bit. On that day, US Airways Flight 1549 departed from New York City's LaGuardia Airport bound for Charlotte, North Carolina, with 155 passengers and crew on board. Three minutes after takeoff, the flight encountered an exceptionally large flock of geese. In the vernacular of the industry, this is called a *double strike* because birds were ingested into both engines, causing them to fail. Captain Chesley B. Sullenberger III was at the controls of the A320 aircraft. Earlier I told you that airplanes glide. With no power, Captain Sullenberger guided the plane over the George Washington Bridge and made what was described by observers as a perfect, wheels-up water landing. The A320 remained intact, vouching for the structural integrity of the aircraft. Passengers were told to brace for a "hard landing" and at impact momentary panic set in, but that gave way to calm and order as the flight attendants took charge of the evacuation, according to numerous reports by passengers. All 155 people on the plane survived with the most serious injuries being broken bones. Captain Sullenberger walked the length of the plane twice in 36-degree water before being the last to leave (Caruso and Franklin 2009; Geller 2009).

The news stories and video clips of this crash and the passengers standing on the wings of the floating A320 waiting to be rescued will be available for years. This story verifies some of the points that I have made repeatedly in this volume: pilots and flight attendants receive extraordinary training, airplanes are built to withstand stressors far beyond those encountered during routine flight, and airplanes can glide for extended distances. Once you take the initial steps to overcome your fear of flying, take a look at the history of Flight 1549.

References

American Psychiatric Association. 2000. *Diagnostic and Statistical Manual of Mental Disorders*, 4th ed. Washington, DC: Author.

Barham, J. 2008. Profiling aviation threats. http://www.securityman-agement.com/article/profiling-aviation-threats-004454 (accessed January 15, 2009).

Barnett, A., and M. Higgins. 1989. Airline safety: The last decade. *Management Science* 35(1): 1–21.

Beck, A. T. 1975. *Cognitive Therapy and the Emotional Disorders.* Madison, CT: International Universities Press.

Bureau of Transportation Statistics. 2008. Airline data and statistics. U.S. Department of Transportation. http://www.bts.gov /programs/airline_information/ (accessed January 14, 2009).

Caruso, D. B., and M. Franklin. 2009. A miracle on the Hudson. *Wilmington (NC) Star-News,* Associated Press, January 16, A1, A4.

CDC (Centers for Disease Control and Prevention). 2007. Impaired driving. http://www.cdc.gov/ncipc/factsheets/drving.htm (accessed January 26, 2009).

Conway, R., and P. Tizzard. 2008. *Flying Without Fear: 101 Fear of Flying Questions Answered.* Surrey, UK: Flying Without Fear Publishing.

Ellis, A. 1994. *Reason and Emotion in Psychotherapy*, Revised and Updated. Secaucus, NJ: Carol Publishing Group.

European Union. 2008. More airlines banned from EU skies over safety concerns. http://www.euractiv.com/en/transport/airlines-banned-eu-skies-safety-concerns/article-177249.

FARS (*Fatality Analysis Reporting System Encyclopedia*). 2007. National statistics. http://www-fars.nhtsa.dot.gov/Main/index .aspx. (accessed January 14, 2009).

FARS (*Fatality Analysis Reporting System Encyclopedia*). 2008. Persons killed, by person type. http://www-fars.nhtsa.dot.gov/People/People AllVictims.aspx (accessed January 16, 2009).

Federal Aviation Administration. 2008. Accident & incident data. http://www.faa.gov/data_statistics/accident_incident/ (accessed January 14, 2009).

Federal Railroad Administration Office of Safety Analysis. 2008. Accident/incident overview. http://safetydata.fra.dot.gov/Officeof Safety/publicsite/Query/statsSas.aspx (accessed January 16, 2009).

Geller A. 2009. A boom and then a jolt as plane lands in river. *Wilmington (NC) Star-News,* Associated Press, January 16, A4.

Hynes and Associates. 1999. Frequency and costs of transport airplane precautionary emergency evacuations. Defense Technical Information Center. http://oai.dtic.mil/oai/oai?verb=getRecord& metadataPrefix=html&identifier=ADA372580 (accessed January 26, 2009).

Jerusalem Post Staff. 2008. El Al named most secure airline. *Jerusalem Post,* February 6. http://www.jpost.com/servlet/Satellite?cid=12022 46330526&pagename=JPost%2FJPArticle%2FShowFull (accessed December 28, 2008)

Mental Health America. 2009. Factsheet: Phobias. http://www.nmha. org/go/phobias (accessed January 15, 2009).

National Institute of Mental Health. 2004. The numbers count: Mental disorders in America. http://www.nimh.nih.gov/health/publications/the-numbers-count-mental-disorders-in-america.shtml (accessed January 26, 2009).

National Transportation Safety Board. 2008. Aviation accident statistics. http://www.ntsb.gov/aviation/Table1.htm (accessed January 16, 2009).

National Transportation Safety Board. 2007. Aviation accident statistics. http://www.ntsb.gov/Aviation/Table5.htm (accessed January 14, 2009).

PlaneCrashInfo.com. 2006. Statistics. http://www.planecrashinfo.com/cause.htm (accessed January 14, 2009).

Reuters. 2006. El Al installs anti-missile systems on passenger planes. http://www.haaretz.com/hasen/pages/ShArt.jhtml?itemNo=683390&contrassID=1&subContrassID=5 (accessed January 15, 2009).

Walt, V. 2001. Unfriendly skies are no match for El Al. *USA Today*, October 1. http://www.usatoday.com/news/sept11/2001/10/01/elal-usat.htm (accessed January 15, 2009).

Wikipedia. 2008. El Al. http://wikipedia.org/wiki/El-Al (accessed January 19, 2009).

Wolpe, J. 1969. *The Practice of Behavior Therapy.* New York: Pergamon Press.

Duane Brown, Ph.D., is a professor emeritus at the University of North Carolina, Chapel Hill, where he taught for twenty-five years. Now retired from private practice, Brown has published twenty-five books and more than one hundred articles and book chapters. He also acted as lead trainer for the American Airlines AAir Born Program, where he led dozens of fear-of-flying seminars.

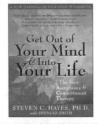